Crossway Bible Guide

Series Editors: Ian Coffey (NT), Stephen Gaukroger (OT)
New Testament Editor: Stephen Motyer

Also in this series

Exodus: Stephen Dray
Joshua: Charles Price
Ezra and Nehemiah: Dave Cave
Acts: Stephen Gaukroger
Philippians: Ian Coffey

Dedicated to:
Rosie – heir with me of 'the gracious gift of life' (1 Pet. 3:7)
Philip and Thomas – our two 'young men' (1 Pet. 5:5)
Godmanchester Baptist Church – 'a people belonging to God'
(1 Pet. 2:9)
R.M. – an elder worthy of 'the crown of glory' (1 Pet. 5:4).

1 Peter: Crossway Bible Guide

Free to Hope

Andrew Whitman

Crossway Books
Nottingham

ISBN 1-85684-086-7

Unless otherwise stated, Scripture quotations in this publication are
from the Holy Bible, New International Version. Copyright © 1973,
1978, 1984 International Bible Society. Published in Great Britain by
Hodder & Stoughton Ltd.

Typeset by Saxon Graphics Ltd, Derby
Printed in Great Britain for Crossway Books, Norton Street,
Nottingham NG7 3HR, by Cox & Wyman Ltd, Reading, Berkshire.

Contents

Crossway Bible Guides

Series Editors' Introduction

Today, the groups of people who meet together to study the Bible appear to be a booming leisure-time activity in many parts of the world. In the United Kingdom alone, over one million people each week meet in home Bible-study groups.

This series has been designed to help such groups and, in particular, those who lead them. We are also aware of the needs of those who preach and teach to larger groups as well as the hard-pressed student, all of whom often look for a commentary that gives a concise summary and lively application of a particular passage. We have tried to keep three clear aims in our sights:

1 To explain and apply the message of the Bible in non-technical language.
2 To encourage discussion, prayer and action on what the Bible teaches.
3 To enlist authors who are in the business of teaching the Bible to others and are doing it well.

All of us engaged in the project believe that the Bible is the Word of God – given to us in order that people might discover Him and His purposes for our lives. We believe that the 66 books which go to make up the Bible, although written by different people, in different places, at different times, through different circumstances, have a single unifying theme: that theme is Salvation.

All of us hope that the books in this series will help people get a grip on the message of the Bible. But most important of all, we pray that the Bible will get a grip on you as a result!

Ian Coffey
Stephen Gaukroger
Series Editors

Note to readers

In our Bible Guides we have developed special symbols to make things easier to follow. Every passage therefore has an opening section which is

the passage in a nutshell

The main section is the one that *makes sense of the passage*. This is marked with a blackboard.

Questions: Every passage also has special questions for group and personal study in a box after the main section. Some questions are addressed to us as individuals, some speak to us as members of our church or home group, while others concern us as members of God's people worldwide.

Some passages, however, require an extra amount of explanation, and we have put these sections into two categories. The first kind gives additional background material that helps us to understand something complex. For example, if we study the Gospels, it helps us to know who the Pharisees were, so that we can see more easily why they related to Jesus in the way they did. These technical sections are marked with an open book.

Finally, some passages have important doctrines contained in them, which we need to study in more depth if we are to grow as Christians. Special sections that explain them to us in greater detail are marked with a mortar board.

How to use this book

This book has been written on the assumption that it will be used in one of three ways:

- for individuals using it as an aid to personal study
- for groups wishing to use it as a study guide to 1 Peter
- for those preparing to teach others.

The following guidelines will help you to get the most from the material.

Personal study

One of the best methods of Bible study is to read the text through carefully several times possibly using different versions or translations. Having reflected on the material it is a good discipline to write down your own thoughts before doing anything else. At this stage the introduction of other books can be useful. If you are using this book as your main study resource, then read through the relevant sections carefully, turning up the Bible references that are mentioned. The questions at the end of each chapter are specifically designed to help you to apply the passage to your own situation. You may find it helpful to write your answers to the questions in your notes.

It is a good habit to conclude with prayer, bringing before God the things you have learned. If you follow the chapters of this book as a guide for studying 1 Peter you will find it divides up into thirty-eight separate studies of manageable length.

Group study

There are two choices:

a. You can take the ten main sections as a weekly/fortnightly study.
b. You can opt for the thirty-eight separate chapters as a weekly/fortnightly study or divide 1 Peter up for yourself using the appropriate number of chapters as a resource each time.

Members of the group should follow the guidelines set out above for Personal Study. It is recommended that your own notes should contain:

a. Questions or comments on verses that you wish to discuss with the whole group.
b. Answers to the questions at the end of each section.

The format of your group time will depend on your leader, but it is suggested that the answers to the questions at the end of each section form a starting point for your discussions.

Teaching aid

If you are using this book as an aid to teaching others it may be helpful for you to note that the material has been divided into ten sections as follows:

Hope for the future	1:1–12
Holiness in the present	1:13 – 2:3
God's people through Jesus	2:4–12
God's people in society	2:13–25
God's people at home	3:1–7
A positive approach to witnessing	3:8–17
The heart of the gospel	3:18 – 4:6
A positive approach to suffering	4:7–19
Grace for Christians at different stages	5:1–7
Grace for Christians in different situations	5:8–14

The sections provide a division of the material in 1 Peter in a way that breaks up the text without destroying the flow of teaching. Each section contains chapters (never more than six per section) which deal with the key points in the text. If the above sections are used it provides a ten week study course. The questions at the end of each chapter can easily be adapted for group use as appropriate.

Background to 1 Peter

Before launching into 1 Peter, it would be helpful to get a background understanding of the letter by asking a few vital questions:

Who wrote 1 Peter?   In Chapter 1 (page 17) you will find good evidence to suggest the apostle Peter wrote this letter. This is the same Peter, also known as Simon Peter, whose life story we read about in the four gospels and the book of Acts.

Peter was a married man (Mk. 1:30; 1 Cor. 9:5) and a fisherman by trade (Mk. 1:16–18). He came originally from Bethsaida (Jn. 1:41). Peter was first introduced to Jesus by his brother Andrew (Jn. 1:41); subsequently called to follow Christ (Mk. 1:17); and soon after chosen to be one of the twelve apostles (Mk. 3:16–19). In fact, he was part of Jesus' inner core of three apostles (Mk. 5:37; 9:2). It seems his future role in the infant church was always going to be central (Mt. 16:18–19). Despite denying Jesus (Mk. 14:66–72), he was eventually restored in his faith and given fresh responsibility to care for Christian believers (Jn. 21:15–19).

The apostle was very much at the forefront in the early days of the Jerusalem church, for example, as preacher – Acts 2:14 ff; spokesman – Acts 4:8 ff; leader – Acts 5:3 ff. He was also greatly used in the early stages of the gospel going to the Gentiles (Acts 10:1 ff; cf Acts 15:1 ff). The second to last time he is mentioned in Acts is in the account of his miraculous release from prison (Acts 12:1–19). Following this, he went to 'another place' (Acts 12:17): this may refer to his ministry among the people to whom he is now writing, in the northern part of Asia Minor.

In the latter part of his life, it seems Peter was based in Rome, from where he wrote this letter (see 'Babylon', ch. 38). According to a fairly reliable tradition from the church leader Clement (1 Clement 5) it appears that he died, along with Paul, in the violent persecution of Christians under Nero that began in AD 64. This would have occurred before AD 68, the time of Nero's death. The story of Peter being martyred upside-down (cf Jn. 21:18–19) in the apocryphal 'Acts of Peter' is almost certainly unreliable.

For whom was 1 Peter written?

According to the apostle, his target audience was Christians 'scattered throughout Pontus, Galatia, Cappadocia, Asia and Bithynia' (1:1): that is, believers in an area that covers most of modern-day Turkey. The order the provinces are mentioned in indicates that the letter was carried on a regular travel route, and therefore reached all the major centres of Christian witness. It is quite likely that copies of the letter were subsequently made and were then distributed to smaller churches in the surrounding areas.

Peter gives us every reason to believe that the churches he wrote to were composed largely of Gentile Christians (note for example 1:14, 18; 2:10; 4:3, 4). Nonetheless, when the gospel was first preached on the day of Pentecost in Jerusalem there were Jewish visitors there from 'Cappadocia, Pontus and Asia' (Acts 2:9 cf 1:1). Some of these must surely have come to Christ and eventually joined up with other Christians in their home area. 1 Peter then, was written to Christians scattered throughout Asia Minor, most of whom were Gentiles, a few of whom were Jews.

When was 1 Peter written?

Our first clue is from early church history: Clement knew of the existence of this letter in AD 96. Therefore, it must have been written before then. The second clue concerns Roman emperors: if Peter died during Nero's reign, as is very likely, his death would be no later than Nero's own death in AD 68. A third clue is found within the letter itself: the hostility faced by Peter's readers seems to be discrimination and abuse on a local level rather than official persecution instigated by the emperor. This would indicate a date of writing no later than AD 64 when Nero began his state-legislated persecution of Christians. The final clue is in the mention of Silas helping Peter in Rome (5: 12–13). It appears from the dating of events in Acts that Silas arrived in Rome some time after AD 62. In summary then, Peter's first letter was probably written between AD 62 and AD 64, about thirty years after Jesus' death and resurrection.

Why was 1 Peter written?   Many Bible students have wrestled with the question 'What specific use did Peter intend for his first letter?' Noticing the basic nature of some of his teaching, they propose two possible answers: First, it may be intended as a kind of catechism, an early church 'discipleship course'. Evidence for this view can be found in the highly structured nature of Peter's teaching in 2:13 – 3:7. Second, others pay attention to the theme of baptism (3:21) and assume this letter was supposed to be used for baptism services: for example, as a sermon on leaving the old life behind and leading a new life; or even as a kind of order of service for baptism (apparently including four hymns!: 1:3–5; 2:22–25; 3:18–22; 5:5–9). Both these possibilities are unlikely, although the first is more plausible.

In fact, Peter explicitly states his purpose for writing as 'encouraging you and testifying that this is the true grace of God' (5:12). God's grace is to be understood properly and experienced in the present tense: 'Stand fast in it' (5:12). This theme explains why Jesus' death is emphasized so clearly throughout the letter. It is the ultimate demonstration of God's grace!

We can gain an even clearer view of the apostle's purpose by noticing his constant references to suffering in 1 Peter. His readers evidently needed to learn how to handle it properly.

Putting these facts together, it is likely that Peter's readers may not have fully realized that a true experience of God's grace does not rule out suffering. There is no immunity from suffering in this life because the world and its inhabitants are still fallen. And when believers suffer there are two dangerous temptations: to opt out of real life in the present and to lose a grip on Christian hope for the future. This may explain why Peter stresses living out our faith in the everyday sphere now and looking forward to our completed salvation when Jesus returns.

The apostle's purpose in writing then, is to highlight God's grace and to prepare Christians to live faithfully for Jesus in the suffering that invariably goes with it.

HOPE FOR THE FUTURE
1 Peter 1:1–12

1

1 Peter 1:1a

First century 'Who's Who?'

Right from the start we need to know who is writing this letter. More importantly, can we take him at his word? Peter begins by introducing himself and stating his authority.

When we write a letter today, we tend to sign off with our name at the end. In the first century the custom was to *begin* correspondence with your name. There is an even bigger difference though between our post today and this letter. Here the writer clearly expects his readers to believe what he teaches and do what he

orders! From start to finish, there is a ring of authority to the letter. So, can we trust its contents? Are we safe in taking the author's word for it? The stakes are incredibly high: affecting the truths we believe and the lives we lead. Peter deals with these questions by introducing himself both as a person and as an apostle. In effect, the authority of Jesus Christ is in operation when he puts pen to paper.

Some people wonder whether 1 Peter was written by the apostle or not, or was it merely put out 'under his name' to increase its credibility? There is evidence to suggest that Peter was the author. First, the author describes himself as 'a witness of Christ's sufferings' (5:1). Second, he seems to have been present during the events leading up to Jesus' death (2:23): Jesus' practice of not hitting back and his trust in God apparently made a deep impression. Third, the author distinguishes himself from his readers in Asia Minor; they have not seen Jesus (1:8). The implication, therefore, is that he has! Also, if 'Babylon'

(5:13) does refer to Rome, as is commonly accepted, Peter was based there in approximately AD 62–64 when this letter was written. Evidence for this location can be found in the writings of two church leaders in the third and fourth centuries: Tertullian (*Against Heretics* 36); Eusebius (*Ecclesiastical History* 2.25.8). For all these reasons, we can take Peter's claim at face value.

Writing tends to have an uncanny way of revealing who we are and what we have been through in life and this letter certainly shows evidence of Peter's hand at work. As a Jew by upbringing, he would be well acquainted with the Old Testament which the author quotes several times and the 'new birth' through Jesus would be familiar to him. The theme of suffering, sometimes when we are in the wrong, would be highly relevant to him too. There are many indications in the letter that could easily reflect the crucible of Peter's life-experience.

On a more down-to-earth note, it is fascinating that the author identifies himself merely as Peter (cf 'Simon Peter': 2 Pet. 1:1). His change of name from Simon to Peter was a direct result of his encounter with Jesus (Jn. 1:42). This experience of 'the true grace of God' (5:12) changed the course of his life. Often in the past and even today people coming to Christ from other religious backgrounds change their names as a sign of their conversion (the origin of 'Christian names'). The impact for us is that Jesus sees us as we will be, by the grace of God – not the unstable people we may currently be, but 'solid rock'. As he opens his letter, Peter can see ahead to what his Christian readers will eventually become, despite their present stresses (5:10).

As we have already seen, this is not just a warm, personal introduction. It is a claim to authority. Elsewhere in the letter, Peter doesn't present himself as superior to those to whom he is writing: other Christians are 'friends' to him (4:12) and in relation to Christian leaders, he is a 'fellow elder' (5:1). However, right from the beginning he describes himself as 'an apostle of Jesus Christ'. Why? Because only someone directly sent by Jesus Christ would have the necessary spiritual 'clout' to write – outlining Christian doctrine and practice in the way he does.

Peter then is one of that unique body of twelve men chosen by the Lord Jesus to pass on the truth about him. For this they received a special measure of revelation by the Holy Spirit (Jn. 16:13). Their words were treated with great weight in a lasting sense: other converts to the Christian faith 'devoted themselves to the apostles' teaching' (Acts 2:42). Some of them too would be used to pen the New Testament Scriptures, for example, the apostle John. Peter's first letter then (like his second) has authority for Christians and churches of all generations and all locations.

The apostle sits down to write realizing that he has the complete backing of Jesus Christ. Anything less would not be enough. For our part, we have to sit up and take notice! This is true whether we are dealing with theological issues like the death of Christ (2:24) or with practical issues such as the way we get on with our boss at work (2:18 ff.). All Peter's teaching in his letter is to be accepted as from Jesus Christ.

Questions

1. Why did Jesus call Peter 'Peter'? (Mt. 16:18). What 'Christian name' would you give to yourself or other members of your group or church?
2. Describe an 'apostle' in your own words. What safeguards do we need to have in speaking about 'apostles' today?
3. Why is it important that the apostle Peter wrote this letter? What would the implications be if he hadn't?

Apostles: then and now

The word 'apostle' in the New Testament is used to describe someone sent with authority to preach the gospel; for example, in the way that an ambassador in a foreign country has his/her government's full backing to speak on its behalf. It comes from the Greek word *apostolos* meaning 'one sent away'.

In the New Testament, the noun 'apostle' is used of:

1. Jesus 'the apostle ... whom we confess' (Heb. 3:1).
2. The twelve apostles chosen by Jesus (Mk. 3:14–19), and also Matthias who was chosen as the replacement for Judas (Acts 1:18–26) and the 'latecomer' Paul (1 Cor. 15:7–11). Teaching in the early church was 'the apostles' teaching' (Acts 2:42 cf Eph. 2:20).
3. Individuals not directly commissioned by Jesus, like the twelve, but sent with authority by the churches as 'apostles'. Examples would be Andronicus and Junias (Rom. 16:7), or unnamed leaders sent from churches with specific missions (2 Cor. 8:23 – translated 'representatives' rather than apostles in the NIV).

In some sectors of the church today leaders are described as 'apostles' – usually referring to pioneers in planting and laying foundations of new churches. How do we assess this? In a positive sense (see 3 above) we can rejoice in the ministry of pioneers sent to help the church grow, but in a negative sense (1 and 2 above) we must be cautious about ideas of 'foundation laying.' This must always rest on the teaching of Jesus and the twelve otherwise we attribute a wrong degree of authority to leaders today.

2

1 Peter 1:1b–2

Strangers on earth – but not to God

We Christians are not always at home in the world. Sometimes we feel distinctly 'surplus to requirements'. However, we are positively wanted by all three members of the Godhead.

Using a familiar Old Testament picture of the 'dispersion' of the Jews, Peter tells us that his readers were literally scattered throughout different parts of Asia Minor (verse 1). Further, they do not really fit into the world they are living in: they are 'strangers' (verse 1). They are like round pegs in square holes: Christians belonging to God in a godless world, and 'strangers' with 'Heaven' written on the front of their passports (Phil. 3:20). They are rather like refugees today who are forced to live in countries other than their own. What an unsettling situation!

This theme of 'strangers' reminds us of the call to live a different lifestyle from those around us. Our way of life involves leaving out some kinds of behaviour, as well as living positively to honour God (2:11–12). It should also show that our stay in this world is a brief one (4:2): when our 'temporary residence permit' runs out we will have to answer to God for our conduct (1:17). On occasions, also, we are made to feel left out – Christians who won't 'join in' are made fun of by those around them (4:4), rather like children in the school playground excluded from playing games because they are seen as 'odd'. We are outsiders – and made to feel it too!

Peter continues with great sensitivity to say that although we may be largely surplus to requirements in the eyes of the world and made to feel it, we are not unwanted in God's sight. In fact, we are 'God's elect', (verse 1: see *Doctrine of 'election'*), chosen and very much wanted by him. And when we speak of him, we are talking of all three persons of the divine 'company': Father, Son, and Holy Spirit (verse 2). Although each have specific parts to play, *all* are involved in our salvation. Emphasize one at the expense of the others and we are likely to miss out. Historically, Bible-believing Christians have emphasized the person and work of Jesus Christ, but in the recent past, there has been a fresh emphasis on the Holy Spirit's ministry and many books have been published highlighting God's Fatherhood. However, Peter stresses the importance of all three persons and so should we!

The Father is the one who chooses us   His specific role is in the area of decision-making and forward-planning. Although this emphasis on 'election' is found elsewhere in Scripture, it presents some Christians with real problems – and mental gymnastics for a few. Practically, though, it is intended to bring security and a real sense of belonging to those feeling 'left out in the cold' in the world at large.

The Holy Spirit is our helper   If the Father chose us to obey Jesus Christ, then the Holy Spirit is the one who gives us the ability to do this. Without his help it can't be done! Because of this divine power, we even become sharers in God's nature, according to Peter (2 Pet. 1:3–4). The basic idea of being sanctified (verse 2) is that of being 'different for God' and having a distinctive lifestyle. It doesn't just have to do with morality: living for God is the key! All of this fits in well with Peter's favourite theme of being godly in a godless world. The practical challenge then is this: are we allowing him to do his work? Are there any ways in which we are hindering the work of the Spirit? (See, for example, Eph. 4:30–31.)

Jesus Christ is the one to be obeyed and the one who cleanses   He is third in order here because the final *goal* of the Father's choosing and the Spirit's setting apart is 'obedience to Jesus Christ'. Calling Jesus 'Lord' (3:15) means obedience on our part, according to Peter. If this is God's aim, then we are called to share it. As 'obedient children' (1:14) we are to become what we are! We have it in us to do what he wants. However, Peter, together with us, knows from painful experience that failure and disobedience are all too possiblc. Lapses of obedience, then, are provided for through the ongoing cleansing of Jesus' blood (cf 1 Jn. 1:7). This is rather like the Israelites who were sprinkled with blood following their commitment to obey God (Ex. 24:7–8). For Christians though, this cleansing is continually available, whenever we need it. A balance needs to be maintained – we are walking a tightrope. On the one hand we should have a deep seriousness about obeying Jesus Christ; on the other a profound realization that we can know God's forgiveness afresh when we fail – all because of the once-for-all death of Jesus on the cross.

In summary then, we are to:

- rejoice that God the Father really wants us for his children
- give the Holy Spirit full room in our lives to make us different for God
- commit ourselves to obey Jesus Christ and yet receive forgiveness if we fail.

Questions

1. *What specific area of obedience is the Holy Spirit working on in your life now? Are there actions or attitudes for which you currently need fresh forgiveness?*

2. *In your own words, how would you describe the different 'jobs' done by each person of the Trinity? Which are you most familiar with, and why?*

3. *Where are there major refugee problems in today's world? What is being done to solve these situations? How do you think it feels to be a refugee? Why is Peter's teaching so relevant to his readers?*

Doctrine of 'election'

God's elect ... chosen according to the foreknowledge of God the Father. (verses 1–2)

This refers to the way God graciously chooses individuals or groups for a specific purpose he decides, for example, Abraham (Gn. 11:31 – 12:7); and, of course, Jesus in a special sense (2:4; cf Lk. 9:35). Groups who are described as elect include Israel (Dt. 10:15) and the church (2:9; cf Mt. 22:14).

God's foreknowledge is an important aspect of 'election'. To some election refers to God knowing in advance who will respond to Christ and therefore choosing them. For others, the idea is stronger; God choosing those he wants without reference to their possible response. The second understanding seems more appropriate, because the first is merely stating the obvious about God's knowledge. Also the word 'know' in Scripture (from which we get 'foreknowledge' here) usually refers to knowing someone personally, for example Jeremiah 1:5, rather than to comprehending facts.

How then should we respond to the doctrine of election? First, it is clearly revealed in Scripture and is therefore a matter of personal trust, even with our mental struggles and questions. Second, it is presented in 1 Peter as a truth for existing Christians; not for preaching to non-Christians. Third, we must keep it in balance with its flip-side: the Bible holds together the fact that although God elects certain people, he still holds human beings accountable for their response to Christ (2:7–8). Fourth, and most importantly, it is a practical and pastoral truth, intended to bring security (verse 1); to encourage obedience (verse 2); and to stimulate worship (verse 3).

3

1 Peter 1:3–5

God's mercy – past, present and future

Our salvation is because of God's mercy. His praise is the end result! It is a salvation for all seasons, spanning yesterday, today and tomorrow.

Having introduced himself and his readers, Peter pauses to pray for God's blessing upon them (verse 2): grace – God's heart in saving us; peace – its result or outcome. These are things we already have through Christ, but still need to experience afresh. God's gifts sometimes need to be unpacked slowly!

Peter begins the main body of the letter by almost bursting into song (cf Paul: Eph. 1:3ff.). Praise is directed to 'the God and Father of our Lord Jesus Christ' (verse 3). Why this description? First, it reminds us of Jesus' unique relationship with the Father (Jn. 20:17). He alone is the eternal Son of God and we are God's children by 'new birth' (verse 3). Second, the word 'god' in Peter's day and ours is very elastic! It can refer to any old 'god'. So how do we know if we have found the true God? – by asking if he is the one revealed in history in Jesus of Nazareth. It is only through Jesus that we trust in God to begin with (1:21).

The apostle's theme from the start is all-round salvation, and the basis for it is God's mercy. It is not like a reward given for work done or a productivity bonus, but, rather an unexpected gift. The only reason for it being given lies in God's generous heart.

Salvation is 'fully comprehensive cover', involving past, present, and future: what he has given us; what he is giving us; and what he will give us. Our testimony then shouldn't just be 'yesterday' centred. It should include fresh examples of God's help and protection 'today' and of the good things we look forward to 'tomorrow'.

Past   Peter states that God 'has given us new birth' (verse 3) and having been born again we can now call God 'Father' (1:17). Other Christians, however remote from us, are part of the same family as our 'brothers' (5:9). New birth was an image first used by Jesus (Jn. 3:1–8) and Paul continued the theme, though somewhat differently, describing the Christian as 'a new creation' (2 Cor. 5:17). It is very relevant today when many people are asking the question 'Can human nature be changed?' Will confining people to prison change their behaviour in the long-term? Why has Communism largely failed in its search for a 'new person'? Humanly speaking, people's characters can be changed to a limited extent, but *only* God can change them in a lasting sense – from the inside out!

Birth of course has lasting effects – ask any parent! Growth follows birth ... Spiritually, the new birth is a beginning, followed by an ongoing longing for God's Word (2:2). So, are we growing on from our spiritual 'birthday', or are we stunted in our growth?

Future   God has given us a 'living hope' (verse 3). Peter now zooms across the horizon to the future 'inheritance' which is awaiting us. As always, biblical hope is sure hope, and not just wish-fulfilment. Because of its firm foundation it does not collapse like a tower made with playing cards, because it is based on the solid rock of Jesus' resurrection! Without this historical event all our hopes lie dashed on the ground (1 Cor. 15:12–19). Jesus is the 'trail blazer', breaking through death for us to follow after. His resurrection gives us living hope! We must be concerned then, when well-known church leaders cast doubts on the fact of the resurrection.

Christians, then, have a secure future unlike investors whose 'securities' can go up or down in value! Our inheritance will not experience decay, and is being reserved for us by God himself. We have hope now of an inheritance then!

Present   We are 'shielded by God's power' now (verse 5). It is all very well to have an experience of God in the past and a home with him in the future, but what about today's difficulties? Peter's readers were currently 'going through the mill' for Christ. The apostle responds in two ways.

First we have God's power to shield us. Our battles may or may not be like those in first century Asia Minor, but we *will* be able to stand daily in the battle until Jesus returns. God's protection is to ensure that we get to our destination safely: he doesn't just 'put us on the bus' and then leave it all up to us!

Second the other side of the coin is our faith. There is no automatic protection! This is rather like a car insurance policy with full cover immediately available, but *we* have to take it out. It is presumption to assume that God will shield us without actively trusting him to do so. Although God's power is a shield, so is our faith (Eph. 6:16).

Our salvation then involves all three members of the Trinity (verses 1–2). It also spans past, present and future (verses 3–5). And the final goal is our completed salvation (1:9). Meanwhile, there is a sense of being 'on the way': our salvation is 'ready' to have the wraps taken off (verse 5). Like a car being put together on the assembly line we are fast approaching the time when the completed vehicle is put on view. Until then we know God's power in changing us and his protection when our faith gets a hammering!

Questions

1. *Is your faith receiving a 'hammering' at the moment? How? What does 'through faith' (verse 5) imply you should do?*

2. *How central is 'praise' to the life of your fellowship? In what ways could praise be 'fuelled' by the truths of our salvation? How could you include stories of God's present help to bring God praise?*

3. *What global issues present a threat to people's hope today? Are people in your country optimistic about the future or not? How is the gospel relevant to those who fear what lies ahead, for example on the international stage?*

Our inheritance

Here in verse 4, Peter uses a word that would have triggered off associations with Israel in the Old Testament period, and God's promise to them of Canaan as an inheritance. For instance God prepared his people for life in the promised land, speaking of it as 'the inheritance the Lord your God is giving you' (Dt. 12:9). However, as we know from subsequent history, God eventually drove his people *out* of their inheritance because of their disobedience. Unlike the inheritance promised to Peter's readers, it was not a lasting one!

So, for instance, while the Christian's inheritance will 'never perish' (verse 4) that of the Israelites was ravaged by invading armies on many occasions (Is. 24: 3–4). Although Peter's readers have a home that will 'never ... spoil' (verse 4), the land of Israel was polluted by the sin of the people (Je. 2:7–8). And the Christian's inheritance will 'never ... fade' (verse 4), unlike the territory of Israel that was often dried up by the drought of God's judgment (Je. 23:10; Joel 1:10–12).

Despite the fact, then, that the vast majority of his readers were Gentiles (that is, non-Jews), Peter uses a number of illustrations and quotations drawn from the Old Testament. The practical implication for us as Christians who are mainly Gentiles is that the Old Testament is now part of our heritage. The apostle will expand on this in 1: 10–12.

4

1 Peter 1:6–7

Tough times: now and later

Difficulties occur frequently and are hard for Christian believers. If we respond positively to them good will come: a proven faith now and a praised Lord later!

Our complete salvation is being kept 'ready' for us (verse 5). Many Christians, though, face real difficulties *now*. Despite being 'shielded by God's power' (verse 5) they are not wrapped in cotton wool! How about those experiences that really test the metal of our faith?

By way of introduction, what do we mean when we refer to 'trials'? In ordinary conversation many people who encounter difficulties say 'This was sent to try me,' reflecting a rather twisted view of God's character. The 'trials' though that Peter is talking about are those that arise solely because of our allegiance to Jesus. They are the price we pay to follow him.

How should we respond to trials?   If we are honest, trials can easily upset us and disturb our sense of peace. Unless we are one of those rare individuals who enjoy suffering, we find it difficult to discover any reason for joy in such experiences. Peter's pastoral advice is wise and practical. Even when we are 'going through the mill' we can rejoice in God's salvation, and the future hope it offers. If we fix our attention on God's grace and the future he has prepared it will help us get through the present 'knocks' with a sense of rejoicing.

What is God's perspective on trials?

Peter begins by showing us that they are only temporary and short-lived: 'for a little while' (verse 6: cf 5:10). When we are stuck in the middle of a tough time, we can often lose our sense of perspective. Our tendency is to become blinkered, focusing only on the 'now', and that looks bleak. The apostle helps us regain our sense of perspective by reminding us of the shortness of life here (for example, 4:2). We are only 'strangers' (verse 1) passing through! Paul, too, spoke from experience in describing troubles that proved to be 'light and momentary' when put on the scales alongside 'eternal glory' (2 Cor. 4:17).

Peter accepts that trials are 'part and parcel' of the Christian life experiences we 'have had to suffer' (verse 6). They are integrally bound up with following Jesus! Like us, Peter's readers were often caught off guard when trials and sufferings appeared (4:12). However, there *is* meaning in our trials. To a certain extent, we share in Christ's sufferings (4:13) by following in his footsteps (2:21). If he suffered in this world it is more than likely that we will too. In accepting this fact it may make trials somewhat easier for us to handle. We can be helped too if we realize that Jesus has gone the same way before us, and is present with us by his Spirit in our suffering (4:14).

What trials does the Christian face?

Peter makes it clear that Christians will face 'all kinds of trials' (verse 6), for example: spiritual (2:11), physical (2:20), and verbal (4:4) (see *Different kinds of trial*). It is worth noticing that Christians are tried in various ways: in different parts of the world, as well as within a local church. We would do well to be sensitive to that fact in attempting to pray for and support our fellow-believers.

How do trials affect us?

Here Peter has some important things to say about our reactions to tough times as Christians, and about helping others in similar circumstances. When trials come, we quite naturally 'suffer grief' (verse 6). However, in practice, the tendency often is to ignore our grief or hide our feelings. Is this a more Christian response? The apostle says 'No!' He recognizes that as human beings we do have real feelings. For instance, there is no need to apologize if you are feeling low after constant 'bombardment' at work all week. However, the biblical response is to be honest about our feelings *and* to find joy in God's salvation. True Christian maturity involves facing our emotions, as well as allowing God to transform them.

Why do trials occur? Perhaps the most common reaction of people going through tough times is to ask 'Why is this happening to me? What is the purpose?' There is nothing worse than going through suffering when there seems to be no meaning behind it or any good to come out of it. For the Christian, according to Peter, trials are never wasted. There is a God-given purpose. We are involved in a process of faith, being refined now, with an end-product when Jesus returns (verse 7).

Firstly then, the process of refining shows that our faith is genuine and not just a 'fair-weather' belief (verse 7). As the heat increases, the gold is increasingly seen to be pure. Trials have a sure way of separating the genuine from the superficial (cf Mk. 4:16–17).

Secondly, there is an even greater purpose in our trials at the end. If we have responded to tough times with faith and joy this will reflect well on the Lord Jesus at his second coming. The fully purified gold will direct praise back to *him*!

Questions

1. *Why should you rejoice during tough times? How can you tell whether your joy is 'put on' or not? Does it help that trials will last 'for a little while' (verse 6)? How?*

2. *How are people suffering in your church right now? Why is it important to face our grief and to help others do so?*

3. *How and where do Christians suffer for their faith: politically (for example, losing their rights); economically (for example, having job promotion halted)? Should we accept this? If not what is the correct way to help our brothers and sisters?*

Different kinds of trial

Peter identifies different trials that Christians are called upon to face.

An abusive world Christians are in a 'no-win' situation, criticized both for doing right (3:16) and for doing wrong (2:12)! They also face verbal sniper-fire for not joining in socially on occasions (4:4) and for being 'religious' (4:14).

Difficulties at work (2:18–20)   Some of Peter's readers were having a rough time at work because of their faith. On occasions they experienced physical violence, which thankfully is legislated against in many countries today. Their temptation was to 'take the law into their own hands' and deal with the boss themselves.

An unbelieving partner (3:1–2)   Christians married to non-believers at best are happily married and yet not able to share their faith with their partner. At worst, there is the struggle of living with an abusive or violent partner, who consistently reacts badly to their Christian spouse's faith.

An attacking devil (5:8–9)   His aim is to 'pick people off', especially when they are vulnerable to attack. This too is a test of faith (5:9). When the evil day comes, the Christian must learn to quickly lift the shield of faith for protection (Eph. 6:16).

5

1 Peter 1:8–9

'Seeing is believing'

Peter had seen Jesus personally. Like his readers, we haven't! However, we are still able to trust him now and know his joy. One day our salvation will be experienced in full.

Having spoken of the day 'when Jesus Christ is revealed' (verse 7) Peter comes back down to earth in his discussion of faith. He focuses on two groups of people who lived by faith without actually seeing Jesus. Two groups of believers who, unlike Peter, had no direct contact with the Lord Jesus in his earthly min-istry: his readers in Asia Minor (verses 8–9); and the prophets in the Old Testament (verses 10–12). Both staked their lives on a Messiah they had never seen first-hand. So what about Peter's readers?

In verses 8–9 the main issue dealt with is the vital connection between faith and sight. Unlike his readers, Peter the apostle had been an eyewitness of Jesus' earthly life (2 Pet. 1:16ff) and sufferings (1 Pet. 5:1). Now both he and his scattered Christian friends were relying on and rejoicing in a Christ they couldn't see. Is it possible to believe in someone without seeing them personally or is the adage 'seeing is believing' true, whether in the first or twentieth centuries? What is the link between faith and sight?

Seeing and believing – automatic faith? For many of Peter's contemporaries at the time of Christ, seeing did not necessarily lead to believing. In fact, 600 years earlier Isaiah had predicted people 'ever seeing but never perceiving' (Is. 6:9 cf Mk. 4:12). In John's gospel, for example, some questioning Jews saw Jesus and yet did not believe (Jn. 6:36), while other Jews came to faith through seeing Jesus and his work firsthand (for example Jn. 9:35–38). Tangible evidence then, has no *automatic* power to force the sceptic into believing! Some years ago, many people were highly excited about the so-called 'Turin Shroud', which was reputed to be the burial cloth Jesus was wrapped in. Even if it were genuine (and it has been proved not to be), there is no guarantee that it would have produced personal faith in those privileged to see it.

Believing without seeing – blind faith?

Peter's main point here is highly relevant to us today, as well as to his readers. For those living in the years or centuries after Christ is it possible to believe in him without seeing him face-to-face? Peter's answer is an emphatic 'Yes!' Despite our not seeing him face-to-face, we *will* see Jesus when he comes a second time at his revelation (verse 7). Meanwhile, we can believe in him on an ongoing basis, having a faith that increasingly grasps our expected salvation. The accusation that could be levelled at Peter's readers and us is that of taking a blind leap of faith, which is how the Danish Christian philosopher, Kierkegaard, described his faith.

Peter's response is fascinating and of great importance: he emphasizes 'you' (referring to his readers) to highlight the *difference* between him and them. Although both currently loved Jesus, only Peter had seen him. Thus the faith of his readers, and ours today, is based on the eyewitness account of Christ given by Peter and his fellow-apostles (2 Pet. 1:16ff; cf 1 Jn. 1:1–3; 4:14). Indeed, it is widely accepted that Peter himself was the main source of information for Mark in writing his gospel.

Our faith then, is based not on our firsthand witness to Jesus, but on that of others. We trust their evidence. However, this in no way means we are reduced to a second-hand, 'borrowed faith'. We still love him, trust him, and rejoice in him. This is regardless of the fact that we have never physically seen him and do not expect to see him until his coming again. An absence of sight does not mean an absence of experience! Indeed, Jesus himself led Thomas and others to understand that 'believing without seeing' was a happy experience (Jn. 20:29).

If we follow Peter's approach, we will avoid two faulty extremes:

- thinking that evidence will automatically produce faith
- feeling that experience is everything regardless of the facts.

His recommendation is a personal, living experience of Jesus based on reliable eyewitness facts. And for those who embrace such a Christian faith, lack of physical sight is no disadvantage!

Before we do see Jesus though, what will our experience be like? Basically, it is a mixture of rejoicing in and receiving from the Jesus we love (verses 8–9). Faith in the 'here and now' is characterized by a joy that defies description and by a salvation we are experiencing more and more all the time. Both our rejoicing and receiving also have a strong future-tense element: the joy is glorious because it is 'the joy of heaven before heaven, experienced now in fellowship with the unseen Christ' (Wayne Grudem). Our receiving means that the goalposts of our final salvation are getting closer and closer all the time. From Peter's perspective we have been saved, we are being saved and we *will be* saved (see *Salvation – past, present and future*).

Questions

1. *Is our experience lacking because we haven't seen Jesus? Where does our joy come from? Why is it 'inexpressible' (verse 8)?*

2. *Peter had seen Jesus (cf 'you have not seen him': verse 8). What does this say about the church's faith through the ages? Is it 'second-hand'? What makes it 'firsthand'?*

3. *'Science says that we should only believe what we can see'. Is this true or not? What are the strengths and weaknesses of this approach to life? How will faith in an unseen Jesus challenge these ideas?*

Salvation: past, present and future

Christians often refer to their experience of God's salvation as 'having been saved', as if it were a past event. For Peter though salvation is more comprehensive. It involves our past, present and future. In fact on the three occasions the word 'salvation' is used it always refers to future salvation (1:5, 1:9, 10).

In the letter as a whole salvation is spoken of, using different terms, in the *past* tense: we have been born again (1:3, 23); redeemed (1:18); purified (1:22); called (5:10); healed (2:24). In short we have tasted God's goodness in all these ways (2:3). Our *present* tense salvation involves becoming increasingly what God intended: the Holy Spirit is sanctifying us in the here and now (1:2) and giving us the power to be holy as God is (1:15–16). Peter's particular emphasis in this letter though is on our salvation in the *future*: receiving salvation in all its fullness. So our salvation is 'ready to be revealed in the last time' (1:5). It is like a future 'goal' (1:9) that is getting closer and closer all the time (cf Rom. 13:11).

Why does Peter talk about 'salvation' wholly in the future tense in this letter? Basically his readers were suffering for their faith and needed to know that the end was in sight. One day their suffering would be over and God would completely restore them (5:10). Peter does not describe our future salvation in great detail: it is like a lasting inheritance (1:4 see *Inheritance*); it is described as 'glory' (4:13; 5:1, 10), meaning that we shall see Christ as he really is, in all the radiance of his character; it also marks the time when God will completely restore us, healing all our 'wounds' from battles on earth (5:10–11). In the rest of this guide future salvation is described as either our full, completed or final salvation.

Salvation is also spoken of by Paul in three tenses: past (Eph. 2:5, 8; 2 Tim. 1:9; Tit. 3:5); present (1 Cor. 1:18; cf Phil. 2:12); future (Rom. 5:9; 13:11; 1 Cor. 3:15; 1 Thess. 5:9).

6

1 Peter 1:10–12

Christ in the Old Testament

The Old Testament is of vital importance for Christians. Its central message is Christ and his work. What greater incentive do we need to look into it further?

Sadly, some Christians today treat the Old Testament as irrelevant, while others believe it is for 'today', but neglect to read it. For Peter, though, it is God's Word for Christians. And if there is any doubt look at how much he quotes from it in this letter! The apostle's teaching here focuses mainly on the prophets and their ministry. It has implications though for how we approach the *whole* Bible.

An inspired Bible The prophets' words were ultimately from the Holy Spirit – 'the Spirit of Christ' (verse 11). They could only speak accurately about future events through his work and the end-product was 'the ... word of God' (1:23). Peter expands on this in 2 Peter 1:19–21 where he states that although prophecy involves men its source is not human: '... men spoke from God as they were carried along by the Holy Spirit' (2 Pet. 1:21). So the Bible is inspired by God himself.

However, it is possible for two misunderstandings to occur in our view of the Bible. First, we may view it as inspired only in the way that men and women are inspired to write good music or literature. Scripture is not the product of human genius. It comes from God: 'from the top down.'

Second though, it is possible to view the Bible's authors (for example, the prophets whom Peter refers to here) rather like God's word-processor keyboard; his Word being 'tapped into them'. In fact the Bible was communicated through real human beings at particular times and places. The prophets themselves were personally involved, speaking, searching (verse 10) and serving (verse 12). They were not just empty 'channels'!

Peter's special emphasis here is on the prophets who predicted our salvation in Christ (verses 10–11). Only God can tell the future without fail (Is. 44:6–7).

A progressive Bible

God's Word wasn't spoken all at once. It was given little by little over the centuries, one piece of the jigsaw following another, and building up more and more of the picture. However, without the coming of Christ the picture would have looked incomplete. So the prophets were not completely sure of the meaning of what they were saying. They understood only in part, and their words primarily served a future generation (verse 12a).

Through them God's purposes were gradually unfolding, until Jesus came and provided the full revelation (cf Heb. 1:1–2). So the prophets spoke with relevance to God's people in their own day *forthtelling*. They also gazed across the horizon as they spoke *foretelling*: there was more to come! For Peter's readers and for us, the climax of the story is known. What was something of a 'mystery' to the prophets and angels (verses 10–12) has been revealed to us. This is a tremendous privilege!

A Christ-centred Bible

God's spokesmen talked of 'the sufferings of Christ and the glories that would follow' (verse 11). Peter clearly believed this to be true, for example, quoting Isaiah's words on Christ's suffering (cf Is. 53 and 1 Pet. 2:22–25). 'Glories' refers primarily to the events following Jesus' death: his resurrection, ascension and coronation (see *Understanding Jesus being 'glorified'* p.136). From Peter's teaching elsewhere, for example 5:1, it may also refer to the benefits *we* gain from his death.

So 'the Spirit of Christ' (verse 11) used the prophets to point to Christ himself at the heart of the Bible. Jesus himself quoted from the Old Testament to reveal who he was during his earthly ministry (Lk. 24:44–47), directing Peter and the other apostles to passages in all sections of the Old Testament 'written about me' (24:44; cf Lk. 24:27). This does not mean that every single verse in the Old Testament is specifically about Christ; rather that the whole 'drift' of the Old Testament points to him!

And if Jesus understood the Old Testament as centring on himself, so should we. So how are we to use Scripture practically in our lives?

A studied Bible The prophets were people of perspiration and inspiration (cf verses 10 and 11)! Having received God's word, they didn't sit back and leave it for a future generation to 'dig into'. They studied it. Inspiration made them Bible students and it should for us too! Their study of Scripture (their own words) involved real effort: 'they searched intently' (verse 10), 'trying to find out' (verse 11) with 'the greatest care' (verse 10). So they were hard-working rather than laid back; precise and not messy: a good example to follow!

Angels too give us a further spur to Bible study. Their strong desire is to 'look into' the gospel (verse 12), a phrase used elsewhere of bending down to see (Jn. 20:5, 11: 'bent over'). Motivation and effort are involved in finding Christ in the Scriptures! How about us?

A preached Bible What the Old Testament prophets *predicted* the New Testament apostles and Christians *preached* – 'by the Holy Spirit sent from heaven' (verse 12). Whenever God reveals himself people tend to speak: the prophets 'spoke'. (verse 10) and 'preached' (verse 12). And through the whole Bible we today are served by prophets and preached to by apostles (verse 12).

The message preached is the 'gospel' (verse 12) of 'salvation' by 'grace' (verse 10) given to us through 'Christ' (verse 11). The power to preach this message is given by the same Holy Spirit who inspired the Word of God to begin with. The book of Acts describes how people filled with the Holy Spirit always spoke boldly of Christ! God himself honours the message of his Son from heaven, and the result is changed lives (1:3, 23). We too can serve others today by sharing the good news in the Spirit's power. And see lives remade!

Questions
1. *How much time do you spend studying the Old Testament? What practical advice would you give to those who find it hard going? What does this passage teach about our own Bible study?*

---

2. *What is your church currently doing to 'preach the gospel' (verse 12)? How are you involved? Why is the Holy Spirit's power essential for outreach?*

3. *People today often try to predict the future through astrology etc. What does the Bible have to say about this? What about those who attempt to predict future trends world-wide?*

Understanding the Old Testament

Peter quotes from all three sections of the Old Testament in his letter:

- The Law (1:16 cf Lv. 11:44–45)
- The Prophets (2:6 cf Is. 28:16)
- The Psalms: (3:10–12 cf Ps. 34:12–16).

Paul also emphasizes that the Old Testament was written for 'us' (Rom. 15:4; 1 Cor. 10:11).

Jesus Christ is the main focus of these quotations from the Old Testament as he himself claimed (Lk. 4:21; 24:44). Matthew in his gospel frequently quoted the Old Testament, presenting Jesus as the 'fulfilment' of Jewish hopes (for example, Mt. 2:17; 4:14, etc.). The writer to the Hebrews speaks of the Old Testament Law and sacrifices as 'shadows' compared to Christ the reality (Heb. 10:1, 5 ff). Augustine wrote:

'the New is in the Old concealed. The Old is in the New revealed'

We should understand the Old Testament by avoiding two extremes:

- Emphasizing that the Old Testament was written for its own day only.
- Reading back into the Old Testament what is not really there.

and by following two guidelines:

- Taking our cue from the New Testament writers, who regularly used a 'stock' of Old Testament verses/passages. How?
- Realizing that not every verse in the Old Testament is directly about Christ. For example, how do we learn about him from the book of Judges? Basically because the message of fallible, temporary saviours looks forward to the ultimate Saviour who is not morally flawed and whose salvation will last forever!

HOLINESS IN THE PRESENT
1 Peter 1:13 – 2:3

7

1 Peter 1:13–16

'Like Father like son!'

Children don't have to be told to mimic their parents. They do it naturally. As God's children we are commanded to imitate him in holiness. This will affect every area of our lives.

Peter's picture here is 'obedient children' and how they are brought up: Christians whose obedience affects every part of their personalities (verse 13) and whose lifestyle is a reflection of their Father's character (verses 15–16). Once their slogan could have been 'ignorance is bliss' (verse 14), but now they know better! More than that, they also have the God-given ability to obey. Through his power they are now 'obedient children'.

The previous section on the prophets flows naturally into this one. The prophets in the Old Testament looked ahead to the coming of Christ – his sufferings and glory. In doing so, their minds were fully engaged (verses 10–11). Similarly we look for his coming *again* (verse 13) and our minds together with our wills and desires, must also be properly focused. Our faith is to impact every area of our lives.

Our minds must be prepared for action The word 'prepare' (verse 13) conjures up a familiar sight in the East. The long flowing robes which people wore in Peter's day often hindered freedom of movement. For the purpose of walking or running they were gathered up and tucked into a belt (1 Ki. 18:46) and then there was liberty to make progress. Christians need to be free to run the race unhindered, as they look toward the finishing tape (cf Heb. 12:1). To that end they must be mentally alert. This is not to say that every believer is called to be an intellectual or even an 'ivory-tower theologian'. Instead we are to be active! Today we might describe it as mentally 'rolling up our sleeves'. This is vital because what we think affects how we live: for instance, downplaying the justice of God will result in over-familiarity with him (1:17). Our thinking then is crucial, especially when our faith today focuses perhaps too much on feelings and experience.

Our wills are to be in harness We are to be 'self-controlled' or literally 'sober'. This does not mean being dull and boring but rather, free from any kind of intoxication that makes us off-guard when temptation or spiritual attack arrives. The aim is spiritual alertness. For example drunkenness is out for the Christian (4:3; cf Eph. 5:18). We are also to be 'sober' spiritually (1 Thess. 5:6–8). Why do we need to be self-controlled? Firstly because time is running out and judgment is on its way (4:5, 7). Secondly because we are in a full-scale battle with the devil (5:8–9) so nothing less than being fully alert will do!

Our desires are to be properly focused Before becoming Christians we were ignorant and lived like it. Our focus then was on our own evil desires. Now we are called to alter our sights in a *decisive* way: to focus single-mindedly on the event of Jesus' second coming and the grace we will receive then (verse 13). 'Grace' often refers to God's motivation in freely giving us forgiveness and new life through Christ. Here it refers to the blessings that lie ahead of us in eternity: for example, complete recovery from the 'knocks' experienced in day-to-day Christian living (cf 5:10–11). Judgment lies ahead for those continuing in 'evil desires' (4:3–5) but grace awaits those who anticipate seeing Jesus face-to-face (verse 13). This is where our full attention should be. Not that we become 'too heavenly minded to be any earthly good', but rather, we should live in the real world of society, work and the family as those who belong to him (2:13 – 3:7).

'Obedient children' then, know that their minds, wills and emotions are all geared 'for obedience to Jesus Christ' (1:2). They are to reflect the character of God in a godless world. Often, the behaviour of a child reflects back on his parents: our lifestyle too reflects the Father we know. To a great extent *his* reputation is at stake (cf Rom. 2:24). We are therefore to turn up the contrast and be distinctive, as he is. Our God is holy. We are to be too! (See *Holiness: God and us*)

The word 'holy' (verse 15) conjures up all sorts of pictures today – often bad ones: people who are 'holier than thou'; a faith so 'out of this world' that it is not grounded in reality; or something for which only Christians in the Superman class need apply. In Scripture, holiness speaks of God being distinctive in terms of righteousness. Morally he is like light with no pockets of darkness at all (cf 1 Jn. 1:5). For us, therefore, holiness means 'being different for his sake' by living rightly. Not being different for difference's sake, but rather being different because we now belong to him. This is an integral part of our calling (1:2) so how does it work out?

Firstly, we are told not to 'conform to the evil desires you had when you lived in ignorance' (cf Rom. 12:1–2). Christians, regardless of denomination, are to be 'nonconformists' in lifestyle, that is, to live differently from the rest of the world. On the positive side we are to be holy in a comprehensive sense, spiritually, physically, intellectually and morally. This command to imitate our Father comes with the full weight of Peter's apostolic authority (verse 15 cf 1:1) and with the backing of the Mosaic Law (verse 16).

Finally, Peter leaves us with two spurs to holiness. First, we can no longer say 'we didn't know' about holiness because Peter points out that the Bible tells us to be holy (verse 16). Second, we now have the resources to be holy: by grace we are 'obedient children' through the new birth (verse 13). The Spirit's work is to aid us in this process of becoming holy (1:2). What he requires *of* us he gives *to* us.

Questions

1. *How much does the second coming of Jesus figure in your everyday experience? In what ways should it affect the way we live? How might this truth be wrongly applied? (cf 2 Thess. 3:6 ff.)*

2. *Some people believe in being 'different for difference's sake'. Why should we reject this motto? What are the reasons why we should be different?*

3. *Christians are to be holy in all they do (verse 15). How will this affect our response to news reports from around the world, for example, on issues such as injustice and Third World debt? Does fixing our attention on Jesus' return (verse 13b) contradict this approach?*

Holiness: God and us

God is 'holy' because of who he is in and of himself. He doesn't just *do* things that are holy! In fact, God would not be God without being holy. He describes himself to Israel as being different from human beings: 'For I am God, and not man—the Holy One among you' (Hos. 11:9). The seraphim in the Jerusalem temple announce him as the one who is 'Holy, holy, holy' (Is. 6:3). Isaiah's response to being confronted by the holiness of God was to acknowledge his own sin (Is. 6:5). God is holy and so is different from the world at large, especially in a moral sense.

God, though, does not keep his holiness to himself! He makes things and people holy – for example, the holy mountain, Zion (Is. 11:9); the holy city, Jerusalem (Is. 48:2); even Isaiah himself (Is. 6:5–7). Above all, his people in both Testaments are intended to be holy. They should be holy because *he* lives among them! For example, the Old Testament quotation in verse 16 (Lv. 11:44–45) emphasizes the fact that a people saved and taken by God for himself are called to be holy. Similarly Peter says God's new covenant community are 'a holy nation' (2:9) as Israel were.

Throughout the rest of 1 Peter the linked ideas of God's people being different *and* morally separate are regularly highlighted. Unlike the world at large, we are 'aliens and strangers' (2:11, etc.). Morally, we do not 'fit in' (4:3–4).

8

1 Peter 1:17–19

Fearing God because of the cross

One incentive to holiness is the fear of God. He is our just Judge as well as our loving Father. However, gratitude for Jesus' death is a further spur to a godly lifestyle.

For Christians serious about holiness, prayer is natural (verse 17). In fact, calling on God as Father is almost 'shorthand' for being a Christian (cf calling on the Lord Jesus Christ in 1 Cor. 1:2). Who though, are we praying to? – an accessible Father and an impartial Judge. Neither one nor the other, but *both*! So how can we as 'strangers' live our lives properly? With a sense of fear because of God's justice (verse 17) and a sense of gratitude because of Christ's redemption (verse 19).

Family life at its best is a great blessing. For some today, the reverse is sadly true. The Christian though, knows God as Father, regardless of his/her family background. God is not only Jesus' Father (1:3) but ours too (verse 17). We are 'obedient children' (1:14), not on our own, but surrounded by other family members (brothers: 1:22; 3:8; 5:9).

One cause of family difficulties can be a breakdown of respect between children and parents. For instance, it is possible to presume on your father's kindness by treating him with disrespect. This can be easier to do when you know you are loved! In the Christian family too, we can be tempted to treat our Father as a soft touch: a kindly 'Dad' who wouldn't harm a fly! Peter responds to this possibility by reminding us that our Father is also our Judge. He is not someone to be trifled with!

Fear because God is judge Peter states that God is judge of both Christian (4:17) and non-Christian (4:3–5). Here in 1:17 he is referring to the accountability of believers at the final Judgment Day. In 4:17 he highlights judgment in the here and now for Christians which is often called 'discipline' (Heb. 12:4–11). Jesus has already borne the full brunt of God's justice for us (2:24). However, we *are* still responsible for our behaviour – now and later on.

Can God the Judge reject us? No! God's family members await *grace* when Jesus returns (1:13); not condemnation and rejection from the family! Our salvation is a result of God's grace from the very start: 'For it is by grace you have been saved through faith' (Eph. 2:8). But the flip side is this: knowing God as Father brings responsibility. How will we be judged? First, we will be judged individually, assessed on our own 'work' (not that of our neighbour). Second, we will be judged with impartiality, because our God 'judges justly' (2:23). There are no miscarriages of justice here and no favourites are given preferential treatment.

Because of this, we need to reject any soft ideas we may have of God as someone we can play games with. He deserves the 'proper respect' (cf 2:17) of fear. This is not the fear of judgment that perfect love drives out! (1 Jn. 4:18) Rather it is a healthy respect and awe towards God from those *within* the family. The Jerusalem church experienced this profoundly in the case of Ananias and Sapphira (Acts 5:1–11 especially verse 11). The early church too lived in the 'atmosphere' of the fear of the Lord (Acts 9:31).

Gratitude because Christ is Saviour The second spur to godly living is that of gratitude to God for Jesus' death. Through that death we have been freed to obey. Peter's readers are no longer 'ignorant' (1:14) about this: they *'know'* that Jesus has redeemed them (verse 18: see *Redemption*).

To 'redeem' means to buy back or to free someone by paying the price for their freedom; for example, slaves could be redeemed and set free. In Peter's day, slavery was commonplace so his picture of Christians being redeemed from their empty lives (verse 18) would have been well understood by the people to whom he was writing, some of whom were slaves themselves (verse 20). Similarly, pictures of people being set free for payment are common today; for example hostages were exchanged in place of arms to Iran; money was paid to free some hostages in Lebanon; soldiers can buy themselves out of the armed forces. Redemption involves paying a price and Peter states clearly that the price paid for our freedom from our former lives is 'the precious blood of Christ' (verse 19).

He describes our former lives as 'empty' and inherited, 'handed down' by our 'forefathers' (verse 18) 'but Jesus has given us our freedom from our past'.

Peter points out that first-century non-believers had empty lifestyles in terms of the gods they worshipped and lived for who were 'worthless' (Acts 14:15) and their thinking about life which was meaningless 'futility' (Eph. 4:17). They led a hollow existence without substance or real meaning. This lifestyle is highly descriptive of many people today!

Through Christ they were freed from their backgrounds. 'Hand-me-downs' are clothes passed down to younger children in a family, that they are often stuck with whether they like it or not! However, freedom from inherited patterns of behaviour and habits is more than possible through Jesus' blood. This handed-down lifestyle could mean the pressure to conform to long-established patterns of behaviour from society at large. It may also refer to the impact of our families on us (Ex. 20:5). We can't naively blame *all* our behaviour on our parents' influence. However, we can be freed from ingrained and inherited habit-patterns that dog our footsteps; to have freedom from the past and its influence on us in the present! But how?

Many situations of hostage-taking and ransoms today involve huge sums of money, occasionally running into millions of pounds. Financial currency was also used in ancient Israelite society: for instance, a worshipper could give a cash payment to the priest in place of his first-born son or animal, freeing them in the process (Nu. 18:15–16). Nothing 'perishable' though can release us from the emptiness of a life without God (verse 18). God himself, in the person of his Son, paid the ultimate price. Peter outlines this fact in terms that remind us of the Old Testament sacrificial system.

Under God's previous agreement sin could be atoned for through the offering of a lamb without any flaw (Lv. 4:32–35; 5:5–6). For us as Christians *Jesus* is 'the lamb of God who takes away the sin of the world' (Jn. 1:29). His absolute purity was essential for the sacrifice (2:22 and 2:24). Because it brings forgiveness (cf Heb. 9:22) his blood is also of infinite value. It is 'precious' (verse 19) and so is he (2:7)!

Questions

1. *What part does healthy 'fear' play in your Christian life/the lives of Christians in your church? Is this a missing ingredient in the church today? How can we change the situation?*

2. *How much does an 'empty way of life' describe the lifestyle of those your church is trying to win for Christ? What will an 'empty way of life' look like?*

3. *Silver and gold are 'perishable' (verse 18). What reception would this truth get from, for example, traders on the money-markets or directors of mining companies? How are Christians to have different priorities?*

Redemption

Like many words used in the New Testament, 'redemption' would have been a familiar word to the people of Peter's day. The Greek language in which the books and letters of the New Testament were written was not 'highbrow', classical Greek but 'street level', common Greek known as *koine*. To Peter's readers in first-century Asia Minor, the everyday meaning of the word 'redemption' would be related to slaves set free or prisoners-of-war released. Two ideas were combined: liberation and 'at a price'.

The background to redemption in the Old Testament can be seen on two levels: nationally it was used of the freeing of God's people from Egypt at the time of the Exodus (Ex. 6:6). Individually in Israelite society, people or things could be redeemed: for example, a firstborn son (Nu. 18:15–16) or property held in mortgage (Lv. 25:25–28). This was no cold and unfeeling idea though: Boaz lovingly redeemed his close relative Ruth (Ru. 4:14). Even more tenderly God *himself* is the redeemer or *goel* (Hebrew) of his people Israel (Is. 41:14 etc).

In the New Testament a vital aspect is Jesus' understanding of himself and his death: he is the Son of Man who came to 'give his life as a ransom for many' (Mk. 10:45). Paul too was fond of this theme (for example Eph. 1:7). Returning to 1 Peter, the price paid is 'the precious blood of Christ' (1:19) and the result is 'freedom' (2:16).

9

1 Peter 1:20–21

Believing God through the risen Jesus

Christ's death is central, but it is also part of a broader canvas. Other events are vital too! Effectively Jesus shows God to us and brings us to God.

Freedom for us as Christians is through the blood of Christ. The cross of Jesus is absolutely central! However, it's not the whole story; Peter puts three other pieces of the jigsaw in place:

Jesus chosen This occurred in God's time-frame, before the clocks of world history had begun, when Jesus and his Father shared 'glory' together (Jn. 17:24). Prior to the days of the prophets (1:10–12) and Noah (3:20), God's choice was made back in eternity! God chose what was most precious to him – his Son. He was the 'chosen ... cornerstone' (2:6) on whom the entire church would be built. He was hand-picked for a specific task – to die for us. In one sense he was the 'natural' choice, being the only person in history without sin (1:19; cf 2:22).

Sometimes people are chosen for assignments today but refuse because the task is too daunting. Jesus, though, was a willing volunteer rather than the Father's reluctant 'conscript' (Lk. 22:42)! He took the initiative to obey the Father: 'I lay it [his life] down of my own accord' (Jn. 10:18).

So God's plan of salvation was prepared before the universe started.

He was not unexpectedly caught out by people's sin. The decision to save had already been taken. It was not 'Plan B'. The cross was the Father's 'Plan A' right from the beginning!

Jesus revealed   Peter speaks of Jesus being 'revealed' (verse 20), that is, being made known or introduced to the world. He describes two occasions on which Jesus has been and will be revealed. Firstly, he was revealed to the world as a new-born baby: 'he was revealed in these last times ...' (verse 20). Secondly, he will be revealed to the world in the future, at his second coming (1:7, 13: cf 1:5; 5:1). In revealing his Son, God is making Jesus visible and known to the world.

God had revealed himself in many ways in the Old Testament (1:10–12). Now he was coming down to us physically in the person of his Son. Visiting the planet! And his coming was in the 'last times' (verse 20) which usually is understood to refer to the period between Jesus' first and second comings. Christ's arrival then signals 'the beginning of the end' for an old world-order. God's genuine 'new age' has dawned!

Jesus exalted   The cross is the centrepiece of God's 'jigsaw' (1:19; cf 2:24; 3:18). It was followed by Jesus being lifted up in two 'movements': from death to life and from earth to heaven. He was raised from the dead and returned to the Father (cf 3:21–22). *Both* events were carried out by God himself. Why? To say a powerful 'Yes!' to what Jesus had done on the cross, and to underline the fact that we can now be 'in the right' with God (cf Rom. 4:24–25). It is vital too that he didn't stay on earth any longer in his glorified body. He returned to the Father in order to send us the Holy Spirit (1:12), assuring us that we belong to God now and giving us solid hope for the future (Rom. 8:15–16; Eph. 1:13–14).

In our lives, we follow in Jesus' footsteps: he suffered and then was glorified (1:11). We too will experience 'eternal glory' after temporary suffering (5:10): the glory of being completely remade as people by God (5:10) and of being given a new, godly environment to live in (2 Pet. 3:13). Jesus has blazed the trail before us.

So the apostle highlights three vital events in God's plan to save humanity: his choice, revelation and exaltation of Jesus. According to Peter, Jesus was chosen, revealed and exalted for *our* benefit: 'for your sake' (verse 20). He is the answer to two of our most basic questions: 'How do we know God is there or not, and if so what is he like?'; and

'Is it possible to make contact with him, and if so how?' Jesus is both the revealer of God and the route to God.

Revealer of God Jesus was 'revealed ... for your sake' (verse 20) to show us what God is like in a way we can grasp. He is the Creator walking his creation. How can we really know what God is like when 'No-one has ever seen God' (Jn. 1:18)? We can only know him through Jesus who said: 'Anyone who has seen me has seen the Father' (Jn. 14:9). To find God and understand his character we need look no further than Jesus.

Route to God Peter says that 'through him you believe in God' (verse 21). He is probably referring to trusting God personally rather than believing in his existence (as in Rom. 1:20). Jesus is the only route to knowing God for ourselves. He makes it clear that God cannot be approached directly; there has to be a 'go-between', and Jesus is that 'way' to God (Jn. 14:6; cf Heb. 10:19–22). So how can we have personal faith in God? – only by approaching him through Jesus. As Christians we offer spiritual sacrifices and praise to God 'through Jesus Christ' (2:5; 4:11).

Jesus then is central as the person who first shows us God and second brings us to God. For our part our faith and hope (1:21) are in God. The last of the famous 'trio', love, is about to come centre-stage (verses 22ff).

Questions

1. How should the phrase 'for your sake' (verse 20) affect you personally? Describe the state of your faith at the moment. How can you ensure it keeps growing? What does faith 'feed on'?

2. Why is it important for our churches to be centred on Christ? What happens if they are not? How can we help those who come to church regularly but have no personal faith in Christ?

3. What 'ways to God' are on offer in our world today? Why is Jesus the only way? How can we explain this to people of other faiths? Is it possible to respect people from other cultures and yet disagree with their beliefs?

Jesus: chosen by God

Two individuals are marked out as 'chosen' in the Old Testament:

David chosen by God as king (1 Sa. 16:1–13) 'my servant whom I chose' (1 Ki. 11:34). David was conscious of God's choice of him (1 Ch. 28:4). Asaph the psalmist also recognized this: God 'chose David his servant' (Ps. 78:70). David then was the servant-king, chosen by God.

The chosen 'Servant of the Lord' Isaiah speaks of this individual as chosen by God. He contrasts the nation of Israel as the chosen servant who had failed God with an individual who would succeed in that calling (Is. 41:8, 9; 42:1; 43:10; 44:1, 2; 45:4). Matthew clearly understands Jesus to be this chosen 'servant' (Mt. 12:15–21).

Jesus himself was aware of being 'chosen' by God. His Father affirmed this openly from heaven at his transfiguration (Lk. 9:35). Even the bystanders around the cross asked him to show that he was 'the Chosen One' by coming down (Lk. 23:35)!

Peter identifies the purposes for which Jesus is chosen by God: firstly he is chosen to redeem people through his death (1:19–20) and secondly he is chosen to found the church (2:4–6). We are 'chosen people' (2:9; cf 1:2) because he was chosen first!

10

1 Peter 1:22–25

Church growth is word growth: seed

We are born into God's family through the Bible. This is a birth with lasting effects. As a result, we are to love each other and spread the word.

Love or truth? This is the choice often faced by Christians and churches today. Go in one direction and you become soft and sentimental. Travel in the other and you could be 'sound, but sound asleep'! Peter's way is better: a balance of love and truth. Truth comes first.

Truth obeyed   Peter begins then, by taking us back to the starting point of our Christian lives: the time when we obeyed the truth of the gospel and purified ourselves (verse 22). The word was preached (verse 25) and we *obeyed*. In talking to non-Christians we often describe people's response to Christ in terms of 'faith' or trusting in Christ. For Peter though, the gospel is both a message to be trusted and a command to be obeyed (or disobeyed: 2:8). It should not be presented therefore, with a 'take it or leave it' attitude. While we must not pressurize people to respond, the gospel is an order from above! For our part we have to make sure it is 'the truth' we are presenting.

Through obeying the truth we have purified ourselves (verse 22). This conjures up the idea of a thorough wash (cf baptism in 3:21). In Old Testament times the Israelites had to go through ritual washings before meeting with God (Ex. 19:10). Jesus spoke of conversion in terms of a bath which has *lasting* effects (Jn. 13:10) and Paul's converts in Corinth 'were washed' despite their filthy pasts (1 Cor. 6:11)! This is a cleansing inside: in the original Greek 'purifying your souls'. What then are the first signs of obeying the truth?

Love shown   If God has become your Father you will have a genuine love and affection for the rest of his children (verse 22): both the kind of love found in a healthy family (the Greek *philadelphia*) and the self-giving love of God himself (the Greek *agape*). Love is something given to us by God as well as something to be developed. It should come naturally on one level, and needs working at on another! However, it cannot be faked. Real Christian love comes from the heart and leaves no room for play-acting. It is a million miles from the kind of 'affection' shown by Judas to Jesus (Mt. 26:48–49). Peter's message about love is: 'You have got it. Now *show* it!'

The thought of family love directs the apostle back to the point of entry into the family: the new birth (cf 1:3). Our love will have staying power because the word which brought us into the family *lasts*! How then does birth occur? Just as human sperm is responsible for human life which lasts a short while (verse 24) so the seed of God's word brings eternal life because Scripture is 'enduring' and 'stands for ever' (verse 25).

For those longing for a completely fresh start in life that is lasting, this image of new birth is powerful, especially as a gift from a merciful God (1:3). However, Peter's quotation from Isaiah 40 shows that it is not just 'turning over a new leaf' (verses 24–25)! It is a brand new start in life from God.

How are people 'born again'? By means of the word of God (cf Jas. 1:18), that is, through the Scriptures, both written (verse 25a) and preached (verse 25b). This word is described in three ways:

The imperishable word   The word of God is 'not perishable ... but imperishable' (verse 23). Peter's familiar contrast is between what is lasting and what is not. Because God's word is imperishable, our future inheritance 'can never perish' (1:4). In many cultures, fruit and vegetables are called 'perishables' because they have a limited lifespan. The Bible, though, has an infinitely long 'shelf-life'!

The living and enduring word   The word of God is 'living and enduring' (verse 23) like its author, the 'living God' (1 Sa. 17:26) and its message, Jesus, the 'living Stone' (2:4). As we proclaim it faithfully we are holding out 'the word of life' (Phil. 2:16). Scripture is also enduring, unlike human beings and the rest of creation (cf 2 Pet. 3:7–10). Its promises have staying-power (2 Pet. 3:13)!

The everlasting word The word of God 'stands for ever' (verse 25). Human beings are upright one minute – the next they are 'on the deck'; flowers are gloriously erect for a while, then they droop and die. In everyday conversation we talk about the lasting effects of people's words, for example, of authors and playwrights 'immortalizing' a person or idea. Realistically though, their influence will not last 'for ever'. But the Bible states clearly that God's word will last for ever and we know that already his words have been faithfully passed down for over 2,000 years.

In our lives faith-sharing must be centred on communicating the word of God, and our lifestyle must back it up (3:1–2). Occasionally, miraculous signs and wonders may confirm it (Heb. 2:4, cf 1:12). But at the very heart must be the word of God: the Scriptures distributed far and wide; the word preached to 'outsiders' (cf 2:10). Peter's final appeal is to remind his friends of their experience: they know all this is true because it happened to *them*: 'And this is the word that was preached to you' (verse 25b). The end product is a life of love and truth!

Questions

1. *What can we learn from Peter's example of knowing God's written Word? How do you think he remembered passages of Scripture? Have you ever tried Bible memory? (Any practical hints?)*

2. *What role does God's word have in your church's outreach? Do you think it needs to be more central? If so, how? Who can preach the word to non-Christians? (cf 3:15 and 4:10–11) What different ways are there of sharing the good news or bringing someone to hear it?*

3. *What recent events world-wide have made people aware that 'life is short' (cf verse 24)? How do people come to terms with this fact? Why is the gospel such good news?*

Old Testament quotations

1 Peter has more Old Testament references than any other New Testament letter except Romans (which is three times as long, with 16 chapters!). These references comprise of straight quotations and Old Testament 'echoes'.

1 Peter	Quotations	1 Peter	'Echoes'
1:16	Leviticus 11:44; 19:2; 20:7, 26	1:17	Psalm 89:26; Jeremiah 3:19
1:24–25	Isaiah 40:6–8	1:18	Isaiah 52:3
2:6	Isaiah 28:16	2:3	Psalm 34:8
2:7	Psalm 118:22	2:10	Hosea 1:6,9; 2:25
2:8	Isaiah 8:14	2:11	Psalm 39:12
2:9	Isaiah 43:20–21; Exodus 19:6	2:12	Isaiah 10:3
3:10–12	Psalm 34:12–16	2:17	Proverbs 24:21
4:18	Proverbs 11:31	2:22	Isaiah 53:9
5:5	Proverbs 3:34	2:24	Isaiah 53:4–5, 12
		2:25	Isaiah 53:6
		3:6	Genesis 18:12
		3:13	Isaiah 50:9
		3:14–15	Isaiah 8:12–13
		3:20	Genesis 7:13, 17, 23
		4:8	Proverbs 10:12
		4:14	Psalm 89:50–51; Isaiah 11:2
		4:17	Jeremiah 25:29; Ezekiel 9:6
		5:7	Psalm 55:23
		5:8	Psalm 22:14

What can we draw from all this?

1. It appears these verses were well-known among many Christians and churches in the first century. They were probably 'part and parcel' of a *stock* of Scripture references. Peter uses them to teach believers who were mainly of gentile origin.

2. The quotations are used to back up or further the apostle's individual arguments. The 'echoes' though, are threaded throughout the letter giving biblical authority to the *whole* message.

11

1 Peter 2:1–3

Church growth is word growth: milk

New birth is only the beginning. Growth follows hard on its heels! We grow up spiritually in two ways: getting rid of sin and taking in God's word. Our motivation is God's goodness.

So far, in 1:22–25 Peter has majored on love within the Christian family. And particularly upon the role of God's word in bringing us into that family. He continues with the same two themes in 2:1–3, but with a clearer focus on Christian growth in *existing* disciples: if the emphasis of 1:22–25 is 'What is the role of the word of God in evangelism?', here it is 'What is the role of the word of God in growth?'

Peter's readers have heard the word (1:25b) and responded obediently (1:22). Regardless of physical age or experience, they have been born again and are 'newborn babies' spiritually (2:2). However, an initial tasting of God's goodness is not enough – we must grow on from this point.

Initially, Peter warns us about sins that will hinder our spiritual growth through the word. God's word has supernaturally produced a genuine love in us for our fellow Christians (1:22). If this is not practised our growth may be stunted and our intake of the word of God affected. We are rather like a garden needing to be cleared of weeds and stones before flowers can be planted and flourish.

Interestingly, the five sins Peter outlines all refer to the way we treat our fellow human beings (verse 1). They are not just 'personal' sins that have no effect on others. Also, they tie in with Peter's emphasis on *truth* and *love* being at the heart of our Christian living (1:22): 'malice' and 'envy' display a lack of *love* – hatred expressed openly and covetousness eating us up on the inside. 'Deceit', 'hypocrisy' and 'slander' display a lack of *truth* – our speech displaying a twisting of the truth, a covering up of reality and a vicious nature too.

So, there must be a measure of purity in our lives, especially in relationships, before taking in the 'pure ... milk' of the word. Practically, this may mean checking our lives before we come together for Sunday worship, in case soured relationships prevent us from hearing God's voice. Individually, our regular intake of Scripture may be hindered because of sin not dealt with. Peter's remedy is to 'rid yourselves' of these sins (verse 1). And the responsibility is *ours*, not God's! The resources though are his (1:2).

Having 'cleared the ground' then, what is Peter's advice positively? It is important to notice that this passage appears to be addressing new Christians in the first instance. However, Peter was certainly aware from Jesus himself of the need to provide for the older 'sheep' as well as new-born 'lambs' (Jn. 21:15–17). God's word is essential for *both*!

The need for spiritual food   Firstly, then, 'newborn babies' display a real craving for milk: you only need to hear the sound of urgent crying or see a baby when it first makes contact with its mother's breast to know that! There is a desperate longing there. New Christians too have a tremendous appetite to learn about God and Jesus: a real 'felt need' for the word of God. This is quite a responsibility for churches in their follow-up of new believers!

The type of spiritual food   Secondly, the kind of intake babies need is vital. Particularly at the early stages of life there is a need to make sure the milk is free from impurity. On my father's farm, the herd of cows are regularly tested for brucellosis for this reason. Why is there such an emphasis on purity? Because only pure 'milk' will produce the purity of life required in the Christian (for example, 2:2; cf 1:15–16). Also newborn babies are unable to handle 'solids' to begin with. New Christians, then, need to have teaching at first that is easily digestible. In the western world at least, it may be necessary to emphasize the reading of God's word as primary, especially with the plethora of good Christian books, tapes and videos available (cf the Bereans in Acts 17:11).

The call to spiritual growth Thirdly, all evidence shows that the vast majority of newborn babies put on weight quite rapidly from birth. With good appetites and a healthy intake, growth and development are natural! God's ultimate goal then is spiritual 'grown ups' – not people who have left learning behind as Christians, but those who display increasing signs of maturity. Their ability to take in God's word should *increase*, progressing from milk to meat, from liquids to solids (cf Heb. 5:11–14). Those further down the road of growth should be role-models for the whole congregation (5:1ff).

The motivation for growth Finally, then, what is our motivation for being growing Christians, hungrily waiting for the next meal? Is it to show what 'first-class Christians' we are? No! Peter's encouragement to clear out the poison of sin and take in the wholesome milk goes back to our experience of God.

In a restaurant, if the starter is tasty the likelihood is our appetites will be whetted for the main course. Likewise, those who have had an initial 'taster' of God's goodness in the gospel will want to experience more as they grow in Christ. However, Peter underlines the fact that growth will never occur without first having experienced God's goodness for ourselves. The first step is to 'Taste and see that the LORD is good' (Ps. 34:8). Everything else flows out from that!

Questions

1. *How was your appetite for God's word when you first became a Christian? What is it like now? Are there any 'blocks' to your regular intake?*

2. *Describe the sins of verse 1 in your own words. How would these sins show themselves in church life? As fellowships, what can we do together to rid ourselves of these things? What about my personal responsibility (for example, hearing slander)?*

3. *The theme of verse 2 reminds us to have concern for starving children throughout the world. Why should we help the hungry? 'It is easier to see physical hunger than spiritual hunger' – What is your response to this quotation?*

New birth

There are three references to new birth in 1 Peter: we have been 'born again' through God's word (1:23); because of this we are 'like new-born babies' (2:2); this 'new birth' (1:3) also involves a living hope for the future.

For Peter, there are two implications:

A new family Through our acceptance of God's word we are born into a new family with God as our 'Father' (1:17); we are his 'children' (1:14); and other Christians are our 'brothers' (1:22; 3:8). The family is world-wide (5:9, 13) and of particular importance for 'scattered' Christians (1:1).

A new nature Without Christ we are all disobedient to God by nature (Eph. 2:1–3; cf 4:3). Even our so-called 'righteousness' is like filthy rags (Is. 64:6). However, through Jesus we are given a new status: declared righteous by God. We are also given a new nature: we are 'obedient children' (1:14). This does not mean we are perfect and have no further need of cleansing (1:2). It does mean we can please our Father (2:5 'acceptable' sacrifices).

The teaching on 'new birth' originated with Jesus (Jn. 3:1–8). Paul, too, taught that in Christ we are a new creation (2 Cor. 5:17). The 'mechanics' of our new birth are a mystery (Jn. 3:8) but it always involves God's word (Jas. 1:18 cf 1 Pet. 1:23) and God's Spirit (Jn. 3:5–6; cf 1 Pet. 1:2). Peter's emphasis is on leaving spiritual babyhood behind and growing into spiritual adulthood (2:2). Perhaps his readers were in danger of stunted growth through not feeding enough on God's word.

GOD'S PEOPLE THROUGH JESUS
1 Peter 2:4–12

12

1 Peter 2:4–5

The church as 'stones'

The risen Jesus is the vital foundation for the church. We too have an important role. Christians are likened spiritually to stones in the Temple and priests offering sacrifices.

Stones can be helpful or unhelpful. One field on my parents' farm is called 'Stony Ground' and it is an unproductive piece of land! Some years ago I worked in Hatton Garden, London – a centre for diamonds and other precious stones. These stones are useful both as jewellery and for industrial purposes. Here Peter calls Jesus 'the living Stone' (verse 4) and us 'living stones' (verse 5). The 'living Stone' is certainly of the precious variety: at least to the Father and to us (verses 4–7). In verses 4–8 the apostle describes three estimates of Jesus as viewed by Jesus himself, God and people.

Jesus' view of himself   Although the apostle describes Jesus as the 'living Stone' (verse 4), this picture did not originate with Peter. He quotes in verse 6 from Isaiah 28:16: 'a stone in Zion', and in verse 7 from Psalm 118:22: 'the stone ... has become the capstone'. Further, he is repeating a theme he first used to the Sanhedrin following Jesus' death (Acts 4:8–12). Crucially, though, Jesus identified *himself* with Psalm 118:22 after telling the parable of the tenants in the vineyard (Mt. 21:33–42). Specifically he linked the killing of the vineyard owner's son with himself as the rejected stone, thus looking ahead to his own rejection and death. Jesus is both rejected and yet vital to the entire construction of the church: without the capstone there can be no building. The crucified and risen Jesus is the only source of salvation (Acts 4:12).

No doubt Peter was with Jesus on this occasion and heard him identify himself with these Old Testament sources.

God's view of Jesus

The Father's view of Jesus is given next. To him Jesus is 'chosen and precious' (verse 6: cf Is. 28:16). He was chosen for his mission before the world was created (1:20), and is precious to God and valuable beyond calculation. Jesus is of *such* value that the Father spoke of his worth from heaven on three occasions during his earthly life (Mk. 1:9–11; Mk. 9:7; Jn. 12:27–29). He is precious to us (verse 7) because he is precious to the Father. Our worship then will be fired by sharing the Father's evaluation of the Son.

The people's view of Jesus

'Men' present another picture – a darker side. Jesus was 'rejected by men' (cf Jn. 1:10–13). In general, people come to him or reject him; their lives are built on him or destroyed by him (cf verses 6 and 8). There is ultimately no middle ground. Peter assures his readers, who are a minority group, that the majority are not always correct. Opinion polls are not always an accurate guide to truth!

What about us? As believing Christians we share God's evaluation of Jesus. Because of this, coming to him is something ongoing – the regular norm rather than the exception. Whatever the world around thinks of him should not influence our perception.

Having described three views of Jesus, Peter turns to the 'church'. How do we view the church Jesus founded? Do churches consist only of 'bricks and mortar': the building itself? What is the role of ministers or 'priests'?

Peter is not afraid to 'mix his metaphors'. He describes the church in Old Testament terms, as both a temple under construction and a priesthood offering sacrifices (verse 5). Christians then, are both bricks in the wall and priests ministering inside! The model Peter uses is the Jerusalem Temple where God 'lived'. He was viewed as unapproachable, except through the priests who acted as 'go-betweens' between the Israelites and God. The new situation which Peter is describing is 'spiritual': he is talking not of bricks and mortar but a 'spiritual house' (verse 5); not of flesh and blood animals but 'spiritual sacrifices' (verse 5).

The church, a Temple under construction God's church then, is a 'Temple' made of 'living stones': the main focus is on *people* who are related to God through Jesus (verse 5). This does not mean that we should despise beautiful 'church' architecture, or be last to volunteer to decorate the church building! Rather that people are at the centre of the church. The church of Christ then, is 'being built' and is still under construction (verse 5). It is not intended to be a massive pile of bricks, but a fully constructed building: every brick integrated and in its proper place; every Christian a part of the whole and using their gifts to serve one another (4:10–11). And the main purpose is *worship*: offering 'spiritual sacrifices acceptable to God' (verse 5).

The church: a priesthood offering sacrifices Peter's second image of the church is that of 'a holy priesthood' (verse 5). He is not referring to the Levites within God's people interceding on their behalf (Nu. 3:5–10), but to *all* God's people having access to him 'through Jesus Christ' (verse 5).

Our God-given identity is as 'a holy priesthood' (cf 2:9). In his eyes then, we are set apart and 'righteous'. We also have something to offer God: our praise and our possessions (Heb. 13:15–16 cf Rom. 12:1; Phil. 4:18). Our sacrifices are both spiritual *and* down-to-earth! And we can please God because through Jesus our offerings gain his approval. So, Christianity is no spectator sport: engaged in by the few and viewed by the many. Watch out for the attitude of 'others doing it for us' – pastors doing all the caring; worship leaders doing all the praising etc. It is also possible to slip into our own form of go-betweens (cf 'priests'): for example we might describe pastors as 'priests'. Or ask the minister to pray for a need because he's perceived as being 'closer to God'. Or treat an individual or group as a spiritual elite with a 'hot-line' to God. He is accessible to *all* of us – individually and together! Jesus Christ is the only go-between we need (1 Tim. 2:5).

Questions

1. *Do you feel a real part of your church family? What 'sacrifices' do you think God wants you to offer to him?*

2. *How do outsiders generally view the 'church'? In what sense is the church a hindrance to faith in Jesus? How does this passage sharpen your vision for your local church?*

> 3. *Why was Jesus 'rejected' in his own day? Would 'rejected' describe people's response to Jesus in your culture today? How would you respond to some from other faiths who claim they haven't rejected Jesus (for example, Muslims who claim to revere him in the Qur'an)?*

The church as 'Temple'

The word 'Temple' is not used by Peter, but the idea certainly is. God's people in his day and ours have continuity with his Old Testament people on a spiritual level. Two temples existed in Old Testament times: the first built during Solomon's reign and destroyed by the Babylonians in 587 BC, the second built after the Jews' 'return' from exile in 537 BC.

In the New Testament the Temple is described in three ways:

Jesus, the living Temple Jesus saw himself as more important than the Temple in Jerusalem which was the centre of worship for the Jews (Mt. 12:6; cf Lk. 21:37). He referred to his own body as God's temple (Jn. 2:19–21): his description of its destruction and resurrection was confused by the Jews with the literal Temple (Jn. 2:19; Mt. 26:61).

Christians, God's Temple on earth Paul speaks of Christians both individually and together as God's temple (1 Cor. 3:16; 6:19; cf 2 Cor. 6:16). The whole church is described as 'a holy temple in the Lord' in Ephesians 2:21.

God and Jesus, the heavenly Temple John records the fact that there is no need for a temple in God's final kingdom 'because the Lord God Almighty and the Lamb are its temple' (Rev. 21:22).

13

1 Peter 2:6–8

The church as 'believers'

Jesus has the effect of dividing people into two 'camps'. Some people share God's estimate of him and believe. Others find their 'downfall' by refusing to believe.

What marks the church off from the world? This is a vital question in every generation. Is there a dividing line? If so, what is it? And how do I know which side I am on? Some today say there is no line really: everyone will eventually be saved. Others would have a very clear line – and claim to know exactly who is either side of it! So what is the boundary between church and world? Significantly, it is marked by a 'stone' – the Lord Jesus. Only this one is not laid by human hands, but by God's (verse 6).

In verses 6–8 Jesus is described as a 'stone' four times (verses 6, 7 – twice, 8).

The 'rejected' stone   Jesus is described as the 'rejected' stone (verse 7b): he, of course, was conscious of this from the beginning and warned his disciples of his rejection (Mk. 8:31), especially by the Jewish leaders of his day (that is, 'the builders': verse 7) who treated him like a useless brick thrown on the skip on a building site and disposed of.

The 'precious' stone   Second, Jesus is described as the crucial stone of great value: the important 'cornerstone' (verse 6) or 'capstone' (verse 7b), the vital foundation of the whole building! The brick has been retrieved from the skip and placed in the central location. Jesus was rejected and crucified by people, but was made the centrepiece by God through his resurrection (1:21).

The 'destructive' stone

Third, Jesus is described as 'a stone that causes men to stumble' (verse 8). Stones can be used for destructive or constructive purposes, for example, to smash windows or build homes. This 'stone' is to be both built on and to be tripped over: to cause the 'falling and rising of many in Israel' (Lk. 2:34). How does this 'stone' divide people? Simply on the basis of their personal response to him. His presence sifts people's allegiances (Mt. 10:32–36): they are either for him or against him.

On one side of the boundary line are believers (verses 6–7a); on the other are non-believers (verses 7b–8). In between is the 'stone' of Jesus.

Believers

One key to being a believer is *personal* faith: trust in Jesus (verse 6) and belief in him (verse 7), not merely head knowledge or church attendance. Another is *specific* faith 'in him' (verse 6): not just having faith in our own faith! It is personal dependence upon the biblical Jesus! As a result you will never be ashamed (verse 6). You will not be embarrassed or disappointed by others viewing your faith as empty and in vain.

Personal faith in Jesus brings a new home too: 'Zion' (verse 6). This is the name by which the Israelites referred to the temple mount in Jerusalem (for example, 2 Sa. 5:7) – however we have come to the *heavenly* Zion (cf Heb. 12:22–24). This stable, lasting home was vital for Peter's rootless readers, many of whom had been forced to leave their homes ('scattered' 1:1).

Non-believers

Non-believers are on the other side of the fence for two reasons: they 'do not believe' (verse 7a) and they do reject him (verse 4) by 'disobeying the message' (verse 8b). 'Don't and won't'! They refuse the invitation of the gospel to 'come' (verse 4) and disobey the command of the gospel too (verse 8). The destiny of non-believers is not made absolutely clear here, only that they 'stumble' (verse 8). The idea is of someone tripping and falling over resulting in their downfall. People who reject Christ do so at their eternal cost. Judgment is awesome (4:18)! In what sense though is stumbling 'what they were destined for' (verse 8)? Are non-believers earmarked for judgment as believers are for salvation (1:2)? No! Peter's point is more general: stumbling is the destiny of all who 'end up' disobeying the message of the gospel. In this life there is still time and opportunity to cross the line (cf 2 Pet. 3:9).

So, Jesus is the boundary-stone between believers and non-believers. We fall on one side or another because of our response to him. People are either built up on him by their faith or fall over him in unbelief. It is a clear dividing-line even though we don't always know who is on either side (2 Tim. 2:19). Eternal destiny is a sobering subject. How can we be sure this is all true? What if it is merely Peter's personal 'hobby-horse'? The apostle's response is to support all he says with the authority of Scripture. He quotes from three passages in the Old Testament to back up his argument with divine authority.

- Verse 6 (Is. 28:16) Isaiah refers to leaders (28:14) who have a false sense of security over their eternal destiny, through an alliance with Egypt. God as judge will show the worthlessness of this pact (Is. 28:17–19). But those who take God's stone for a sure foundation will 'never be dismayed' (Is. 28:16): their security is in God.
- Verse 7 (Ps. 118:22) Here the psalmist shows the difference between the builders' false evaluation of the stone and God's true evaluation. His has staying power!
- Verse 8 (Is. 8:14) God now describes *himself* as the stone. Two responses are possible: either finding true safety by fearing him alone or stumbling and falling over him. Many take the latter path (Is. 8:15).

All three passages underscore Peter's message with God's authority. His teaching about Jesus, and about belief and unbelief can be entirely trusted.

Questions

1. *In what sense is Jesus 'precious' to us as Christians? Do you find this word sentimental-sounding? If so, what expression would you put in its place? Why is he of tremendous value to you?*

2. *How much does the Old Testament figure in your church life? When was the last time you heard a sermon from an Old Testament book? Why does Peter quote it so much here?*

3. *Non-believers (verse 7) must have heard the gospel. Where in the world today would you be most likely to find those who have never heard? As a world-wide church, what is our responsibility to them?*

14

1 Peter 2: 9–10

The church as 'people'

God's people today are rather like Israel yesterday. Through his mercy we have been made into a nation with an amazing status. And our purpose is to bring God praise through our lives.

Loneliness and isolation are common experiences today and many people feel 'left out'. Peter's readers certainly knew this. They were separated from one another distance-wise (1:1), were 'outsiders' in the world and made to feel it (4:4)! These things cannot fail to influence how people view themselves. The world's message of being 'unwanted' has its impact. Jesus received the same message: he too was 'rejected' (2:4). He coped by knowing his true identity as chosen by God and precious to him. We too may be treated by the world as surplus to requirements, but we *are* wanted by God.

Peter begins by contrasting the stumbling of non-believers (verse 8) with the status of believers (verse 9). In describing the church as 'people' he uses three Old Testament sources: Exodus 19:6; Isaiah 43:20–21; and various verses from Hosea. He addresses the church as a whole congregation – not just a collection of individuals. Our status as believers has four components, previously used to describe God's people Israel.

'A chosen people'   Israel was chosen by God out of sheer love (Dt. 7:7–8). Sadly, she failed to live up to her calling. God's name was slandered because of her behaviour (Is. 52:5). She failed to serve God faithfully. Jesus, however, was the proper Servant, 'chosen by God' (2:4). Through our oneness with him, we too are 'chosen people'. This shouldn't produce pride in us: we are chosen because of his 'mercy' (verse 10). And the fact of being chosen should stimulate praise in us (verse 9), not intellectual problems!

'A royal priesthood'   Kings in the ancient world often had their own priests, who enjoyed the privilege of being close to the king. As Christians, we belong to *the* King, having access to him at any time. As priests we also have something acceptable to offer. We don't come empty-handed! First we bring our praise (verse 9), then other 'spiritual sacrifices' too (2:5 cf Heb. 13:15–16). Peter is not informing us of this just to boost our self-esteem. However, he *is* encouraging us to see ourselves as God does: rather than being on the rubbish-tip we are to see ourselves as in the royal palace!

'A holy nation'   This does not mean just a morally pure people but rather a people who belong to God in a way that others don't. We are God's 'special property', belonging to him and no-one else. Our relationship with God resembles the marriage ceremony where both partners agree to 'forsake all others' for each other. It is a special relationship. Interestingly, a common picture for Israel's unfaithfulness to God was 'adultery' (Je. 3:8): Israel failed to be set apart for him alone. Naturally, a holy nation will lead holy lives (1 Pet. 1:15–16), free from the growing sin of 'nationalism' because we are part of God's new 'nation', and not merging into the crowd morally, but standing out for him (1 Pet. 4:3–4).

'A people belonging to God'   Christians do not belong to the world (verse 11). Where *do* they fit in? People today often try to trace their roots, especially if, for instance, they have never met their natural parents. The church's roots are simply in belonging to God. Our 'belongings' are precious to us and they go wherever we go. Often we are not too keen to share them – they are 'ours'. God is somewhat like this with us: we belong to him and therefore are special to him.

Why has Peter outlined our status as Christians like this? Is it to make us feel better in a lonely world? Not primarily! God's clear purpose is to bring himself praise, through us 'publishing abroad' what he has done for us in Christ. In the last analysis salvation is God-centred and the praise goes to him (1:3). Declaring his praise means worship upwards and witness outwards although the difference isn't always that clear-cut! (Acts 2:11)

Our praise then flows from what he has done for us (verse 9). Spiritual darkness was our natural habitat (Eph. 4:18), but he has now moved us to a new home with brilliant lighting! God deserves the credit because he caused all this to happen. Our worship and praise may be stilted and our witness sometimes quiet, because we don't sufficiently realize who he has made us and what he has done for us. If we did, our lips would open more quickly!

Finally, Peter alludes to the book of Hosea (verse 10) to show what we were and what we are now, by God's mercy. Hosea's tough calling was to take back his unfaithful wife Gomer as a sign of God's faithfulness to sinful Israel (Hos. 3:1–5). Their two children were Lo-Ruhamah (meaning 'not loved': Hos. 1:6) and Lo-Ammi ('not my people': Hos. 1:9). By God's grace the people's situation was reversed and the Israelites became again his 'loved people' (Hos. 2:23). Although they were Gentiles, Peter's readers had also experienced this shift, from being unloved outsiders to dearly-loved insiders. For us, comparing what we were with what we are now is guaranteed to encourage praise.

Questions

1. What good does looking back as a Christian (verse 10) do for you? How are we in danger if we don't? (NB: see 2 Pet. 1:5–9, especially verse 9.)

2. Why does Peter emphasize the church as 'people'? How can our churches avoid the danger of becoming impersonal? What effect should these two verses have on the way we see ourselves as fellowships?

3. Why is nationalism so common today (i.e. stressing the 'rights' of our own people against someone else's)? Is it possible to have national pride without being guilty of nationalism? How is the church to be different as a 'nation'?

15

1 Peter 2:11–12

Abstinence is a virtue?

We are to be in the world but not of it. Our godly lifestyle should be attractive and gain people's attention. Not to bring us praise, but God!

A popular British television series, *The Good Life*, featured two couples: the snobs with their materialistic lifestyle and their neighbours, the Goodes, trying to return to a simpler, non-materialistic lifestyle living off their own resources. Attempting to live 'the good life' won them little praise from their neighbours! The Christian lifestyle, too, always evokes a response from those around, whether positive or negative. In verses 11–12 Peter recommends God's version of 'the good life' where the neighbours cannot help but praise God when they see the Christian lifestyle, even if they were critical before.

Jesus clearly taught that we are 'in' the world but not 'of' it (cf Jn. 17:15 and 17:14, 16). Christians live 'among the pagans' (verse 12) and are involved like them in families, jobs, etc. so 'the good life' is not an attempt at escapism! (NB: 1 Cor. 5:9–10) However, believers are to 'abstain from sinful desires' (verse 11) and not join in with their neighbours' wild living (4:3–4). This is quite a tightrope to walk, avoiding the extremes of compromise on the one hand and retreating from the world on the other!

In these verses Peter effectively builds a bridge linking the two main parts of his letter. 1 Peter 1:1 – 2:10 focuses mainly on what God has made us, both individually and together. From 2:13 onwards he discusses the practical outcome of this. Right now we are *on* the bridge: stretching from beliefs on one side to practice on the other. How solid is the bridge at each end? It is possible to be either too academic or too practical about our faith.

Peter uses four pictures or images to describe Christians living 'the good life' of God.

Temporary residents

Peter describes Christians as 'aliens and strangers' (verse 11; cf 1:1, 17). Refugees, sadly, are a common sight today: people uprooted from their own countries and living in another country for a while. Should they try and 'fit in' ('When in Rome do as the Romans'!) or attempt to be different to keep their identity? Peter's response for Christians is:

- Don't attempt to be the same morally (4:3–4)
- Do make sure you are not deliberately awkward though! (2:16–17)
- Remember you are temporary residents here (2:11).

Time is short (4:7) and our complete salvation is on its way (1:9). The Christian must 'live the rest of his earthly life ... for the will of God' (4:2).

Fighting soldiers

Peter warns about 'desires, which war against your soul' (verse 11). Becoming a Christian ends one war (for example, see Eph. 2:14–18) and begins another: our sinful desires start attacking our souls. The sinful nature and the Spirit clash with one another (Gal. 5:16–18). The war is on two fronts: 'a war on wants' (verse 11) and 'a war of words' (verse 12). We will look at the second later.

The 'war on wants', our sinful desires, is largely unseen; it is an internal battle and more difficult to fight because of that! Conflicts too can produce battle-weariness: but we are not to wave the white flag of surrender to sin (Heb. 12:3–4). How about those who fall in battle morally? Christians don't shoot them, but try to 'restore' them – just like our God (1 Pet. 5:10; cf Gal. 6:1).

Beauty consultants

Peter urges Christians to live 'good lives' (verse 12). The Greek word for 'good' literally means 'beautiful' or 'attractive'. Fashion and beauty are popular today and they were in Peter's day too (1 Pet. 3:3–4). Our Christian living is to be attractive, having magnetic drawing power for outsiders and making them sit up and think (3:15)! Words on their own are not enough (cf 3:1–2). Our behaviour then is being judged by the world around for its beauty. If outsiders find it attractive the first question will be 'Where did you get that from?' Then praise goes to the 'manufacturer'! Non-Christians know a good thing when they see it despite their initial criticism. The eventual result brings glory to God and not us (cf Mt. 5:14–16).

Defence Witnesses   'They accuse you of doing wrong' (verse 12). Christians are 'in the dock,' being falsely accused of 'doing wrong' (verse 12). In actual fact we are in a 'no-win situation' because they criticize us even when we are doing right (1 Pet. 3:16; 4:4)! In the first century believers were accused of: being cannibals (Christ's 'body' was eaten in the 'Lord's Supper'); immoral behaviour (at their 'love-feasts'); breaking up families (through some becoming Christians); disloyalty to Caesar (because Christians claimed that 'Jesus is Lord'!). And today? Non-Christians are not slow to point out the moral failings of Christian leaders. We are sometimes accused too of destroying people's cultures by sharing the gospel with those of other faiths. And in a local community outsiders are quick to say: 'I never thought a Christian would behave like that.'

When accused, our initial reaction is to defend ourselves with words and try to clear our name! Peter's antidote is life not words (verse 12; cf 2:15). The most effective way of dealing with opposition is living 'the good life'!

Non-Christians may continue to accuse in this life, but when God visits in person it will be a different story. He will be glorified through our having lived 'the good life' (verse 12).

Questions

1. *Peter says our lifestyle should be seen. How should this work out positively? What is the danger here?*
2. *As local churches, how can we strengthen each other in the battle against sin? What help would you give to someone who has 'fallen' morally?*
3. *Church leaders are often accused (verse 12) of 'trespassing' in the political realm by for example, commenting on issues in society. Are those criticisms fair? What convictions lie behind them?*

Handling verbal abuse

Peter frequently mentions abusive words thrown at Christians from outsiders: for example, in 2:12; 2:15; 3:9; 3:16; 4:4; 4:14. Clearly, verbal abuse is hurtful – we are still human! And Proverbs talks often of the powerful effect of words: for good or for harm (for example Pr. 12:18).

Peter outlines two types of hurtful words: accusations, presumably for specific things (2:12; 3:16); insults and abuse which were probably more general (3:9; 4:14; 4:4). Words are spoken against good behaviour (3:16) and bad (2:12)! At root, they come out of sinful hearts ('malice' and 'slander' – 2:1 cf 3:16). Our response is not to trade insult for insult but rather we are to overcome evil words with good (3:9 cf 2:23). We are also to carry on living in the right way. This will silence people (2:15) and may also open their lips to praise God (2:12)!

For Christians, part of our witness is the use of our tongue (see *Use of the tongue*, 1 Pet. 3:8–12).

Finally, it is important to note that these are accusations of an 'informal' nature. Believers are not literally 'on trial'. When wrongly accused on a legal level, self-defence is quite appropriate: for example, Paul's 'defence' before the Jews (Acts 22:1) and King Agrippa (Acts 26:1).

Inner conflict for Christians

Here Peter talks about the battle inside: the realm of our desires and our souls (verse 11). His way of dealing with these desires is total abstinence. For an alcoholic who has given up drink even a small drop is dangerous! And for the Christian who has 'done with sin' (4:1) it is the same. One sin can lead to another and another.

Sin is past tense for the Christian. He/she is in a new era. Temptation remains but there is a new energy to say 'No!' *and* to live lives of obedience through the power of the Holy Spirit (1:2). So evil desires belong to the time we knew no better (1:14). Specific sins are to be 'dumped' (2:1). The battle is subtle too: we can even use our Christian freedom wrongly to conceal evil (2:16). So Peter urges a decisive break with sin and evil desires (4:1–2). Even elders must fight against such temptations as greed and 'bully-boy tactics' (5:2–3).

The closest parallel to this passage is Galatians 5:16ff in which Paul describes the conflict between our sinful nature and the Holy Spirit. The 'fruit' of both are obvious (compare Gal. 5:19–21 and 5:22–23) and victory is gained through realizing our death to sin with Jesus (Gal. 5:24) and by living in the power of God's Spirit (Gal. 5:16).

GOD'S PEOPLE IN SOCIETY
1 Peter 2:13–25

16

1 Peter 2:13–15

Christians in society – submission

It is possible for Christians in society to be seen as troublemakers. After all, they follow a higher authority. However, they must 'fit in', as far as they are able. For God's sake!

Can there be 'Ostrich Christians' with their heads buried in the sand? Only the most obscure groups of believers in history have managed to withdraw completely from society. While Jesus' followers are 'aliens and strangers' (2:11) they are also called to live in the so-called 'real world', bringing praise to God by living out the good life (2:12). We may not be of the world, but how do we live *in* it?

Firstly, the key to the good life is found in the word 'submit' (verse 13): in society at large (2:13–17); at the workplace (2:18–20); in the home (3:1–7); and within the church family (5:5). Submission is not guaranteed to find many buyers in today's largely anti-authoritarian world!

Secondly, the political situations we live in nowadays may well be different from that in the Roman Empire of Peter's day, but the themes of politics remain essentially unchanged. A few wish to impose their views on others whether by democratic or undemocratic means. However, whatever political situation we live in, Peter calls on us to submit 'to every authority instituted among men' (verse 13) bearing in mind the God-given principles that Christians are called on to uphold.

Thirdly, elsewhere in the New Testament Jesus and his disciples were regularly accused of being subversives: 'stirrers' in society, and creators of civil unrest! Jesus himself was accused of not paying taxes to Caesar and claiming to be a rival 'emperor' (Lk. 23:2; cf Lk. 20:20–26; Mt. 17:24–27). Paul and his team in Thessalonica were accused of defying Caesar's decree by preaching Jesus as God's anointed king (Acts 17:3, 6–7). When Paul was in Jerusalem he was charged, among other things, with being 'against Caesar' (Acts 25:8), despite appealing to him (Acts 25:11)! Allegiance to a higher authority was clearly a threat to the powers-that-be.

With these things in mind, how should we as Christians live in society at large?

What are we to do?   'Submit' is the key (verse 13)! Two different Greek words are used in 1 Peter for submission and this is the weaker of the two. It is not the same as the level of obedience to Christ which is required of believers (1:2). Nonetheless it is a proper deferring to and recognizing of society's leaders. We are to make up our own minds to do this as part of our discipleship ('submit *yourselves*': verse 13). Submit – yes; 'press-ganged' – no! As Christians in society, we are to show 'proper respect' (verse 17). Just because we are Christians doesn't make us rebels for rebellion's sake! We are to fit in as far as we can.

Who are we to submit to?   Peter says that we are to submit to 'every authority' (verse 13) from the person 'at the top' to those at the grass roots: from the Prime Minister or President to the lowest local official (verses 13–14). And Peter was writing this letter during the harsh reign of Nero from AD 54–68 (although before the 'short, sharp shock' of persecution in Rome for Christians in AD 64.) The reason Peter says this is because he believes in God's sovereign hand in society: he institutes the authorities (cf Rom. 13:1–7), with the specific purpose of discouraging bad behaviour and encouraging good behaviour (verse 14) for *everyone's* sake. God's care extends beyond his own people.

Where will the benefit be seen?   The benefit of submissive Christians in society is threefold. First, it is for God's sake (verse 13). It is part of our everyday discipleship and honours him. His will is paramount (verse 15) and he is the one Christians are to serve and fear (verses 16, 17).

Second, it is for society's sake as a whole. Through our co-operation, leaders in society will be encouraged to fulfil their God-given role, making the world a better place for everyone to live in. If the authorities don't, however, follow God's 'job description', they will find themselves answerable to him. Third, for the sake of unbelievers. They may, and do, criticize us for our behaviour (verse 12) but this is one sure way of silencing their criticisms (verse 15)!

How can we apply this to our situations today? Positively, our co-operation in society is a form of worship: it is 'for the Lord's sake' (verse 13). But where do we draw the line? The issue of 'civil disobedience' is certainly one for debate in our own day. For example, some pacifist believers in Britain break the law by withholding a proportion of their taxes from the government: the same proportion that is spent on defence! Hard and fast rules are impossible on complex issues. Peter's emphasis though is this: as far as you are able, live as a 'good citizen'. However, as a free person you can claim a higher allegiance if and when the crunch comes. Don't be deliberately rebellious though!

Questions

1. *What will 'doing good' (verse 15) in society mean for you as an individual Christian (for example, your attitude towards authority; your practical response to authority)?*
2. *Why is the God-given role of authorities (verse 14) so important? Does verse 14 describe all authorities? If not, what does it mean? How do you think God will treat authorities who don't do what God wants?*
3. *As a church, locally and nationally, what issues are high on the political or social agenda now? How do you feel about submitting to government legislation on these issues? What can you do to voice your agreement or disagreement?*

Christians and the authorities

Peter's attitude to the state and the authorities clearly has a positive 'ring' about it. Is this true elsewhere in the Bible?

Jesus essentially taught a constructive view of the state. When the religious and political leaders attempted to trip him up concerning taxes (Mk. 12:13–17) he affirmed the rightness of giving Caesar what was legitimately his and God what was his too! He also practised what he preached by paying his taxes although in an unusual way (Mt. 17:24–27)! The authorities, then, have their proper place, as long as they don't usurp God's.

Paul, too, spoke about the same theme in Romans 13:1–7. Some teaching parallels that of Peter, for example, God's role in instituting authorities and his purpose for them. However, he also stresses fear of punishment to discourage Christians from breaking the law (cf 1 Pet. 4:15). Further passages remind us of the priority of praying for the authorities (1 Tim. 2:1–4) and of submitting to them (Tit. 3:1–2).

The other side of the coin is also found in the Bible when people defied the authorities on spiritual grounds. Daniel and his three friends disobeyed the Babylonian authorities at great personal cost when asked to compromise spiritually (Dn. 3 and 6). The earliest Christians refused to obey human authorities by stopping preaching Jesus (Acts 4:19), obeying God rather than men! And in Revelation 13 John portrays the state as an enemy of God's people and an ally of the 'beast' – Satanically-inspired government!

Scripture then is generally positive – but not without qualification. The key question to ask is: 'What *sort* of lead are the authorities giving morally and spiritually?'

17

1 Peter 2:16–17

Christians in society – freedom?

Freedom is at the heart of the gospel. It can, however, be used or abused. Genuine liberation involves serving God and respecting others. Live it out!

The gospel means freedom. After all, one of the words used of salvation, redemption, refers to slaves set free (see 1:18 *Redemption*). In Peter's day there were a massive number of slaves in the Roman Empire, all with little or no rights at all. There were some among the Christians to whom he was writing (2:18): still slaves, but free in Christ. Freedom though, for them and for all Christians, is not always easy to handle.

Freedom grasped   Some years ago an elderly man was captured and kept hostage for five years in Lebanon. His release was greeted with great joy. For himself though, he appeared unsteady on his feet after his time in captivity. Freedom can affect our sense of balance. Former Eastern Bloc countries are now learning to live without Soviet domination, and many are finding the first taste of freedom difficult to handle. For Christians too, the freedom that comes from trusting Christ sometimes means a while 'finding our feet spiritually'!

Freedom abused   Peter begins then by underlining our identity – in Christ we are 'free men' (verse 16). We must therefore live out what we are. As a wise pastor, though, he realizes the danger of Christian freedom being abused, for instance using it as 'a cover-up for evil' (verse 16), rather than living a life that is above reproach. How then would Christian believers have justified this kind of behaviour? The argument could go something like this: 'God my Father (1:17) is the supreme authority and judge. Jesus my Saviour is seated at his right hand above all authorities (3:22). According to Paul, I'm there too (Eph. 2:6)! So why bother about obeying the speed limit? I'm above all that!' Freedom can easily turn into licence. Liberation can go to our heads in the wrong way. As Christians we are called to be obedient to human laws as long as they do not conflict with God's laws.

From Peter's letter we can see that abuse of freedom could occur in a number of ways: 'free' citizens thinking themselves above the law in some way (verses 13–15); 'free' employees 'doing wrong' by misusing their employers' time (verse 20); 'free' wives dominating their husbands (3:1); 'free' husbands liberated to be inconsiderate to their wives (3:7). There is a strong grasp of freedom – but a poor application of it!

It is not only Christians who can misunderstand their freedom. Society for its part can add to the problem by portraying us as rebels for the sake of it. In some situations they may think we claim allegiance to a higher power in order to evade our responsibilities on earth. Non-Christians will be watching to see how we handle our freedom. Our good behaviour, though, should act as a 'silencer' drowning out all such comments (2:15).

Having talked about abusing freedom though, Peter's remedy is not a dose of legalism. He doesn't encourage slavishly following 'the rule book'! No, we are to live as free people by serving God and others.

Freedom demonstrated   How then is our freedom to be demonstrated? Simply by living as 'servants of God' (verse 16). At one time freedom in society at large was typified by the slogan 'Do your own thing!' According to Peter, that kind of lifestyle carries us away like a flood (4:4): *it* is in control of us. True freedom is a far cry from that. The Christian's slogan is 'Now you can do God's thing!' We have the ability to do what we know to be right which is real freedom. And so Christ's liberating death makes us free to 'live for righteousness' (2:24). In fact, we are 'slaves to righteousness' (Rom. 6:18). What a paradox – freedom and slavery hand-in-hand. Doing what God wants brings genuine liberty!

How then does this work out in practice? We express our freedom in two ways: by serving God and respecting people. The ground rule is to have 'proper respect for everyone' (verse 17). It is to be appropriate to the person it is given to: for instance, the way we treat God and our fellow-Christians will be quite different. Our respect is also to cover everyone, without discrimination. No-one is to be outside the orbit of our respect: non-believers as well as believers; little-known Christians as well as 'famous' ones; the Prime Minister as well as God (verse 17).

Peter goes further with *specific* instructions (verse 17). Respect for fellow-Christians means showing them God's quality of love, not just a friendship love but something far deeper and more sacrificial: a real family love (cf 1:22; 3:8). Concerning our relationship to God and the king, Peter quotes Proverbs 24:21 with a slight but significant difference. There both God and the king are to be feared. Here the king is to be honoured (a weaker verb!) and God feared. Why is this important? Simply to underline the fact that our allegiance to God is primary. The king comes after God. 'First things first!'

Questions

1. *Why does Peter describe us as 'free' and 'servants'? How do the two fit together? What does it mean to be free? Can we be free and bound by anything?*

2. *Biblically, what lies behind Peter's teaching on 'respect', in terms of beliefs about the character of God and the nature of human beings? How should this affect our attitudes towards, for example, non-Christians, those of a different race or gender?*

3. *What legal or moral 'cover-ups' have been revealed in the media over recent years? How were they discovered? What can we learn from them?*

Christian freedom

According to Peter, freedom is what we are ('free men') and what we have ('freedom': verse 16). This theme is prominent in the New Testament. It refers primarily to freedom from the penalty, power and eventually presence of sin; and freedom to love and obey God through Christ.

First, true freedom is promised by Jesus. He declares himself Messiah at his home synagogue in Nazareth by proclaiming freedom for prisoners (Lk. 4:18; Is. 61:1). To his fellow Jews he offers freedom indeed to those who will face the truth and him (Jn. 8:32, 36). Ultimately, this freedom comes through his death (Rev. 1:5).

Second, Paul speaks of freedom as a present possession for Christians: through Christ! Because of our union with him we are freed from sin and are now slaves to righteousness (Rom. 6:7, 18). Elsewhere he talks of 'the freedom we have in Christ Jesus' (Gal. 2:4).

Third, freedom in its fullness is our destiny – and that of the currently-groaning, fallen creation which will one day be liberated from decay and be 'brought into the glorious freedom of the children of God' (Rom. 8:19–21). For us our future freedom involves seeing Jesus as he really is (cf 1 Cor. 13:12) and being perfectly like him (1 Jn. 3:2).

Fourth, what about freedom now? Galatians 5:13–15 is a short passage with striking parallels to Peter's teaching. In Paul's chapter as a whole, believers are urged to stand firm in freedom (Gal. 5:1) and to use it properly (Gal. 5:13). Both legalism and licence are dangers for Christians. Freedom means staying free in Christ, and yet using our freedom in a proper way.

18

1 Peter 2:18–21a

Christians at work – employers

The workplace plays a large part in our lives. As Christians it can be a positive place or difficult place. Our awareness of God should make us good 'employees' whatever.

Where is the church from Monday to Friday? For most people it is 'at work'. If you add up the time spent weekly by the average Christian in church activities you will find it is far less than the 40 hours (plus travelling time?) spent at work. A quarter of our time at least is spent in the workplace. For some of course the home is their place of work. Others may be in the difficult situation of having no paid form of employment. Whatever the case it is not surprising that Peter tackles this important area for Christians. The wider society (2:13–17) is the first arena for 'the good life' (verse 12). The work place is the second!

Of course, there are many differences between Peter's day and ours. The common factor though is this: the workplace marks the intersection between Christian living and a largely non-Christian world. It is where our Christianity really counts. While conversion changes *us* radically, it may not change our boss! We cannot leave God 'outside' our factory, office, shop, home, place of further education; our faith is to engage with everyday life. The workplace is not always 'the last stop before heaven': it is sometimes a place of real suffering for Christians.

The bosses Peter is referring to here are probably not Christians though Paul writes to a Christian 'boss' in his letter to Philemon (cf Eph. 6:9; Col. 4:1). In terms of how they treat their workers there is a wide variation. Peter talks of two kinds of employer:

'Good and considerate' (verse 18)

They have the welfare of their staff at heart. Going to work is an enjoyable experience!

'Harsh' (verse 18)

This literally means 'crooked' or 'bent'. They are morally dishonest and evil. This is true of the world at large: a 'corrupt generation' (Acts 2:40). Employers today may also be crooked in terms of pay, conditions, expectations, etc. but the Christian is not to behave like this.

Realizing that there are a variety of bosses delivers us from two extremes: naively thinking 'I'm a Christian. Everything will be fine at work'; and cynically thinking all employers are the same rotten bunch. God's image is still visible in part – in those who are good and considerate more than in others who are harsh.

What then may the temptation be for an employee with a crooked boss? It could be to 'straighten him/her out'! Doing this is to respond wrongly. Peter's advice is to submit in general *and* in this situation. Submission is a familiar thread throughout 2:13 – 3:7. Unlike 'submissions' in wrestling, it is voluntary! The idea is always used in the New Testament of our relationship to an authority, for example, Jesus to his parents (Lk. 2:51); citizens to the government (1 Pet. 2:13), church members to leaders (Heb. 13:17); Christians to God (Jas. 4:7), etc. It refers to a proper acceptance of the authority placed over us. This does not mean, by the way, that the person submitting is inferior or of less value. There is no need to 'downgrade' ourselves.

If we are learning to submit to God (1 Pet. 5:6) this will affect the whole of our lives, including work! What is our attitude to the boss? How do we respond when he asks us to do something? At root, our attitude should be positive and our actions co-operative (but cf Joseph and the boss's wife! Gn. 39). What about harsh bosses who treat us badly, even when we're doing the right thing? It is obviously easier to respond well to a good employer but Peter calls on us to respond well to both (verse 18).

With a crooked boss the temptation is to attempt to change him. After all, it is his fault you are a bad employee! Or is it? Peter's message is: Be changed yourself – submit! Our responsibility at the end of the day is for *our* actions and not those of others. They will have to give an 'account' of their own behaviour to God (4:5) and judgment belongs to him (2:23).

So how should we respond to the 'harsh' employer (verse 18), dealing out 'unjust suffering' (verse 19) even to the point of 'beating' (verse 20)? Assuming it is not your fault, Peter's advice is to 'bear up under the pain' (verse 19) by taking your eyes off the pain and on to God (cf Jesus: 2:23). You may not get proper treatment from your boss, but you will be commended by God.

Applying this teaching to our own day is not easy. The master–slave relationship is not an exact parallel to the employer–employee one. And many countries also have detailed employment laws. What Peter cannot be saying here is that we are to passively 'lie down' under every bad experience at work. In cases of grievance, companies usually have procedures to follow. There may be legal protection for unfair dismissal, sexual harassment, etc. These exist for Christians too! However, we don't live in an ideal world. Some Christians in difficult work situations may be called to 'stick with it' rather than changing jobs for example; all with a firm eye on the Lord and pleasing him. It is living out 'the good life' in a world that is far from good!

Peter has no explicit advice here for Christian bosses. Paul does though (see Eph. 6:9; Col. 4:1; Philemon), stressing that they too have a responsibility to treat their workers with fairness and without threats. We all have a Master in heaven to answer to (1 Pet. 1:17).

Questions

1. *Have you ever been treated unfairly by an employer? How? Why? What was your response? What should it have been?*

2. *What does it mean to be 'conscious of God' at work? Will this conflict with concentrating on the job?*

3. *How do people suffer at work in your country generally and as Christians? What kind of employment laws do you have? How can the law prevent some of the worst features of Peter's day (for example, 'beating': verse 20)?*

Unjust suffering

Here Peter compares suffering that is deserved (verse 20a) with that which is undeserved (verse 20b). Although it was unjust, the latter was what Jesus experienced and it is part of our calling too (verse 21). What does Peter say about 'unjust suffering' (verse 19)?

Christ – the model of unjust suffering   Christ is the example for us of how to handle unjust suffering (2:21, cf 2:23). In his lifetime he was without sin (verse 22), and yet he experienced suffering (verse 23).

- At his trial insults were thrown at him, but he didn't respond in like manner (verse 23).
- In his death his sufferings were, strictly speaking, 'unjust'. He bore *our* sins (2:24); he died for us 'the unrighteous' (3:18).

Christian suffering   The reasons for suffering are   wrongdoing, for example, 'doing wrong' (2:20a) at work; criminal behaviour (4:15); 'right' behaviour, for example, 'doing good' (2:20b); suffering for Christ (4:14, 16).
Types of suffering are   words – for example, good behaviour maliciously spoken against (3:16); deeds – for example, a beating from your employer (2:20).

Handling unjust suffering   Because it is unfair the natural temptation is to pay the person back by 'taking the law into our own hands'. Peter's way is to commit yourself to God (4:19 cf Jesus: 2:23) and keep doing good (4:19). Remember the example of Jesus too (2:21)!

19

1 Peter 2:18–21b

Christians at work – employees

Many Christians work for somebody else. If so, they are to be good employees, whatever their boss's response. And if that involves suffering, God will show his approval.

'I'm really being persecuted at work/school' says your fellow-Christian at housegroup. Your response may be to feel there is more to it than meets the eye! In the previous section we focused on 'bosses' – how they treat Christians in the workplace and what we should do to respond properly. Ultimately, it has to do with the

focus of our gaze: towards him/her or God? Now we come to the people Peter is directly talking to – 'slaves'.

But why does Peter talk to slaves and not 'masters' here? Firstly because his readers were generally drawn from the ranks of employees rather than employers (cf 1 Cor. 1:26). Secondly, because Christians generally were often regarded as 'rebels' for accepting a higher authority than the emperor. So in this shaky situation, Christians had to watch their step at work and do everything possible to prove themselves good employees for Christ's sake. This may be timely advice for Christians in politically unstable parts of the world today. It has a bearing on all Christians everywhere though.

If there are two kinds of non-Christian 'boss', there are also two kinds of Christian employee: those 'doing wrong' and those 'doing good' (verse 20). This is not quite so clear-cut in practice, but is helpful as a guideline. While all Christians are called to live in a godly way, this can't always be taken for granted. Those 'doing good' are to carry on, whatever the boss's response and will be commended by God (verse 20). For those 'doing wrong' the message is quite different. The fact that they have to endure suffering is their own fault and, therefore, their suffering does not bring a commendation from God (verse 20).

Reasons for suffering   For Christian employees suffering at work the obvious question is: 'Why?' Am I going through this just because the boss is difficult? Is he making an example of me as a Christian? Alternatively, is it my own fault; for example, am I suffering for being consistently late for work; shoddy workmanship; interfering with other people's work (cf 'meddler': 4:15); using the boss's time to witness to my workmate. These result in a bad reference from God as well as your employer. It is a quite different issue from, for example, being given an unfair volume of work by your boss because you are a Christian and regarded as a 'soft touch'.

Response to suffering   What then is our responsibility? It is to please God by 'doing good' at work, whether it pleases our fellow human beings or not. Work is an important part of our service to God. First, however, we must check it *really* is pleasing him. If we suffer for what is right he will give us an excellent 'reference' – 'it is commendable before God' (verses 19, 20b). God himself will give his own 'medal for faithful service' in our jobs, his 'Well done!' (cf Mt. 25:21).

But if we find out we are suffering for the *wrong* reasons (verse 20), what then? Realizing it is the first step! Ridding ourselves of the sin (2:1) is the second: there is always fresh forgiveness for those willing to admit their faults (1:2) and change their behaviour.

The flip side to our responsibility at work is God's presence there. He dwells in people who spend a large proportion of their time in the workplace. This is not 'the secular world' for Christians. It is made sacred by God's involvement.

First, we are to be conscious of the Father when receiving unfair treatment (verse 19) and his response will be to commend us. He is the ultimate person to bring our work grievances to, and the ultimate person to write us a 'reference'. He is actively there.

Second, Christ's example is also important (verse 21). He carried out the Father's 'job description' (Jn. 17:4) and suffered in the process. Jesus has been this way before and that must be an encouragement. We are called to 'follow in his steps'.

Finally, although the third member of the Godhead is not specifically mentioned here, being different for Christ is impossible in any sphere without his help (1:2). And according to Paul, submitting is one result of the Spirit's control in our lives (Eph. 5:18–21, especially verse 21). This is crucial for a slave when told to submit (verse 18).

So, Father, Son and Holy Spirit are with us at work. They are not left outside when we arrive at work and collected again when we leave. All three persons are 'there' when you wake up. And they are as much 'there' later on when you are dealing with a difficult customer on the phone or when the boss is breathing down your neck! ... For our part we need to:

- check we are suffering for the right reasons
- keep our eye firmly on God and his approval
- 'bear up under the pain' (verse 19).

Questions

1. *How will this passage affect your witness at work this week? What might change in your attitude or actions? What needn't change?*

2. *Is the idea of God's approval 'foreign' to us as Christians and churches? If so, why? How and when will he 'commend' us?*

3. *What major forms of 'unjust suffering' are you aware of in our world today? Why are people treated badly because of their race, colour etc.? How can Christians help to combat this?*

Slaves in the first century

The word translated as 'slave' here comes from the Greek word *oiketes* not *doulos*. It refers particularly to 'household slaves'. In terms of our language today, this indicates a position higher than 'slaves' but lower than 'servants'. How were these 'slaves' regarded?

They were generally well-treated (cf verse 20)   Slaves were not just unskilled workers, but also what we would call 'professionals' (teachers, managers, doctors). They were well catered for under Roman law and sometimes were paid for their services. 'Freedom' could eventually be purchased (cf 1:18–19).

They had no choice in their slavery   If you were born a slave you had no choice but to be one. Your social standing would be lower than most, and financially you would be poorly off. Actually it is significant that Peter addresses slaves at all. In similar codes of behaviour in Peter's day (for example Jewish, Stoic) only masters were addressed. To society generally, slaves were not full people and had no rights at all.

The issue of slavery itself was never directly challenged by the early church. Society was not democratic and Christians had little opportunity for voicing their views. However, it was subtly undermined, as illustrated by the story of Philemon and Onesimus (NB Paul's letter to Philemon). Here Paul stands the idea of slavery on its head by introducing the more important reality of Christian brotherhood. The legal abolition of slavery came through Christian social reformers in the nineteenth century. In every generation though, the Christian church should be free from social prejudice (for example, see Gal. 3:28).

20

1 Peter 2:22–25

Jesus: our example in suffering

Suffering is central to Christian living. Jesus is our example – in suffering for the right reasons and handling it properly. However, we can never copy his unique suffering on the cross.

The word 'Copycat' is often used negatively of those who have nothing original to say or do. Peter's picture of imitating Christ, though, is positive – even in suffering. His discussion of this theme expands his previous teaching on suffering at work (2:18–20). In tackling the subject of Christ's 'example' he goes right back to the cross. The two cannot be separated. Following in Jesus' footsteps is all bound up with experiencing the gospel to begin with. Peter poses two questions:

The 'Why?' of suffering   For us the basic reason is that: 'Christ suffered for you' (verse 21). This phrase does not refer to his suffering for our sins on the cross (as 2:24). Rather, the meaning is the sufferings he faced during his lifetime. He is our example, both in the reasons for suffering and in the way to handle it.

Suffering is tied up with our calling as Christians. Jesus experienced it on the path to glory (Lk. 24:26). We too have been called to 'eternal glory in Christ' (5:10) by the same road! Not viewing suffering as intrinsically good in itself, but instead going through it in the way Jesus did. Mimicking him. Tangible examples are always an encouragement. They make us aware we are not alone (5:9). Here Christ himself is the example – a high standard, but possible to emulate. Peter gives two pictures of how we learn to 'copy' Christ:

1. By following his 'example' (verse 21): children often learn the alphabet by copying a sheet provided by their teacher. To get it exactly right they use tracing paper, and produce an 'example' from the original work. Christians don't suffer exactly as Jesus did or for the same reasons, but he does provide us with a pattern to follow in our response to suffering.
2. By following 'in his steps' (verse 21): people and animals often 'leave their mark' when travelling through mud or snow. We can 'track' them by following their footprints. Jesus has gone before us and we can plant our shoes where he has already been.

Jesus, then, is our model for suffering. Peter has already said there is no credit in suffering for the wrong reasons (verse 20a). Jesus' sin was not the reason for his suffering because he committed no sin (verse 22 quoting Is. 53:9). Neither should it be ours! And for Jesus there was no saying one thing and doing another. Word and deed matched up perfectly. He was consistent even while suffering. We are to check that our feet are going firmly into his 'tread-marks'!

The 'How?' of suffering
The most natural thing to do when suffering unfairly is to fight back. Following Jesus, though, means two things:

1. Not returning fire (verse 23a): Insults are often met with a dose of the same medicine (3:9) and if this doesn't work, the next step is usually threats: 'I'll get even some day!' This is not Jesus' way!
2. Entrusting ourselves to God (verse 23b): How do we entrust ourselves to God? Jesus didn't look *across* at his enemies but *up* to his Father. He suffered injustice humanly but appealed to a 'higher court of law', to God, the impartial judge (1:17). This was not a cold legal appeal though; but a warm entrusting of himself to the Father. And for us? Peter doesn't recommend venting our anger when wronged or burying it inside us. We are to give ourselves repeatedly into God's hands (verse 23b). He can 'take it' when we express our real feelings.

Peter goes on to talk about Christ's sufferings in a way we could never 'copy': his death for us (verses 24–25). Significantly, he includes himself: 'He ... bore *our* sins' (verse 24: author's emphasis) despite addressing his readers as 'you' prior to and following this statement (verses 21 and 25).

Peter's thoughts here are based on Isaiah 53:12. Jesus had nothing on the debit side of his 'account' with God (verse 22) and yet our sins were registered there and paid for. The account was totally closed through payment of death. We can liken Jesus' action to that of a 'stand-in' at the theatre: an actor steps in and takes complete responsibility for someone else's part. Christ 'stood in' for us, but this was no 'play-acting'. He bore God's wrath against our sin (cf 2 Cor. 5:21).

This was not merely a 'spiritual' event though: it occurred 'in his body', in real human history. But why the 'tree' rather than the cross (verse 24)? To Peter and his fellow-Jews it would be familiar as a reminder of the curse of God's judgment against sin (Dt. 21:23). This curse was totally removed through Christ (Gal. 3:13)!

Jesus died as our 'stand-in' to remove this curse and bring us forgiveness. Also his death was intended to change our lifestyle: the debt of sin was cancelled and the boss of sin was buried! Christians should therefore regard themselves as dead to sin but 'alive and well' to righteousness (cf Rom. 6:11). So there is no forgiveness *of* sin without freedom *from* sin. Both were Christ's specific aim!

The second part of verse 24 together with verse 25 also quote from Isaiah 53. Firstly, Peter describes the healing effect of Jesus' death (verse 24: cf Is. 53:5). Paradoxically, the wounds of one person bring healing to many! 'Healed' here is used in a spiritual sense (cf Mt. 8:17 where the same verse is quoted with reference to Jesus healing physically).

Secondly, Peter likens us to sheep who have wandered and got lost (verse 25: cf Is. 53:6). Morally and spiritually we were like wayward sheep each going our own way. Now we have returned to the 'Shepherd' who gave his life for his sheep (Jn. 10:11, 14) and to the 'Overseer' who will watch over us from now on.

In summary then we are called to copy Christ in the way he dealt with suffering during his lifetime. However, we could never imitate his 'once for all' (3:18) suffering on the cross. He alone is sinless (verse 22) and only he could die for our sins (verse 24). And his goal is to forgive us, change the way we live and 'bring us home' to God.

Questions

1. *Our calling is to suffer but do we have to go looking for suffering? Why?/Why not? Is Peter just thinking of persecution? What other kinds of suffering might he have in mind?*

2. *What does it mean for your church to have Jesus as its 'Shepherd and Overseer'? How will this work out in practice? Why are elders described in a similar way (5:2)? Is there any significance in this?*

3. *God 'judges justly'. What is your opinion of organizations like the 'United Nations' who seek just solutions to disputes throughout the world? How fair are they? To what extent should we as Christians support them and how?*

GOD'S PEOPLE AT HOME
1 Peter 3:1–7

21

1 Peter 3:1–2

Christians at home: submissive wives.

The behaviour of a Christian wife is part of her discipleship. It will involve genuine respect for her husband. This will win non-Christian husbands more effectively than words!

One real-life situation in the church today is that of Christians married to non-Christians. Often in practice it is the wife who is the believer. This throws up all sorts of questions for the Christian: what level of commitment should I give to the church (for example, my time, money, etc.)? How about our children's upbringing (if we have them)? And most importantly: will my partner ever become a Christian? Peter begins with this question but he doesn't end there. His discussion broadens out into tackling Christian marriage generally.

What about marriage partners who 'do not believe the word' (verse 1; cf 1 Cor. 7:12–16)? How had this situation come about? Perhaps the Christian partner had come to Christ while already married or had married a non-believer while at a low ebb spiritually. Alternatively the Christian spouse may have been ignorant of the Bible's teaching on this issue prior to getting married, or could even have married a non-Christian because of a shortage of suitable Christian partners. The 'norm' of course is for two believers to be joined in Christian marriage (2 Cor. 6:14). However, Peter is a realist: it doesn't always work out that way.

Peter begins with a general command to wives, one that applies whether the wife is married to a Christian or not: 'Submit!' (verse 1). This fits in with his teaching so far (2:13; 2:18). And for a model to follow they need look no further than Jesus (2:23). Submission within marriage does not mean total, unquestioning obedience, whatever the demands. It does involve loyalty and unswerving commitment. Paul gives similar teaching to Christian wives in Ephesians 5:22–24. This is not just Peter's 'hobby horse', but an important aspect of the teaching of the early church.

To us at the end of the twentieth century, talk of submission (verses 1, 5) and obedience (verse 6) has a rather 'old-fashioned' ring to it. Are Christian wives being called to be holy 'doormats'? Certainly not! Peter had firsthand experience of married life and took his wife with him when he travelled (1 Cor. 9:5). Here he portrays submission as the path of true beauty (verses 3–4) and true spirituality (verse 5: 'put their hope in God').

Having touched on submission generally, Peter now examines the particular scenario of a 'mixed marriage,' specifically a Christian wife married to a non-Christian husband. Clearly, the Christian woman is not immune from Peter's teaching just because her partner is not a Christian. In fact, her behaviour is even more vital! The first concern of anyone in this situation will be to see their partner 'won over' to Christ, then they can share together at the deepest level (verse 7).

Peter describes the non-Christian partner in greater depth and how to win him for Christ (verses 1–2). The same principles of course apply in the reverse situation of a Christian husband married to a non-Christian wife.

A partner described   It is obvious that the non-Christian partner described here has heard the gospel ('do not believe the word': verse 1). He may have heard it, for example, through his wife's testimony; 'Guest Services' at the church etc. However, the term used by Peter indicates a sense of *active* disobedience: a rebel with his fist in the air, rather than an unbeliever just shrugging his shoulders. How can such a person be won to Christ – by Christian books cunningly left around; cassettes poised to be played; discussions initiated? Words, words, and more words! In this particular situation, that is not the solution.

A partner converted   It is worth saying that Peter's general approach to evangelism is word-centred. The preached message is the seed that will produce lasting fruit (1:23–25). When asked about this message, the Christian is encouraged to give a spoken response to the enquirer (3:15), not merely to point to his/her behaviour! New Testament faith-sharing then, is primarily a matter of proclaiming the message. In *this* situation though, words have failed to have the desired effect. If the ground is so hard that it refuses to take any more water, it is better to turn the tap off for the time being!

Here, then, is the encouragement that non-Christian husbands can be won to Christ through lifestyle, via the message lived out before their eyes, twenty-four hours a day, seven days a week. And what will they see? A different way of behaving: with purity and reverence (verse 2). A genuine exhibition of Christian character that affects how the Christian wife responds to her husband and which flows from her 'bended knee' to God.

Peter affirms then the desire of the Christian partner to win their spouse for Christ. However, he also recommends a change of strategy. We may not be in the exact situation outlined by Peter. However, there *are* principles to learn about faith-sharing: our evangelism must be centred on sharing the message of the gospel (backed up, of course, by a consistent lifestyle). This is not always easy with those close to us, who know us through and through: for example, relatives, close friends. There may be occasions where words lose their effect and we have to communicate by just living out the message.

People are at times won to Christ by this method (although it is not a foolproof one that works every time).

Questions

1. *Are there people close to you personally for whom words of witness have run out? How do you feel about keeping quiet? What else can you do to win them?*

2. *How many people in your church are married to non-Christians? What are their special needs? How can we best support them in practical ways and get alongside their partners?*

3. *What is the general state of family life in your country? In what sense is Christian family life a part of our witness? How does it compare with family life in general? What similarities and differences are there?*

Non-Christian partners

God's express will in both Testaments is for his people to marry 'within the family'. The Old Testament for example, warns of the pitfalls involved in 'mixed marriages': one reason for King Solomon's downfall was his foreign wives and the 'gods' they imported via marriage (1 Ki. 11:1 ff.).

In the New Testament a very different situation is faced, that of one partner in a marriage relationship coming to Christ *after* being married for a time (1 Cor. 7:12–16): here the apostle Paul recommends that they stay with their non-Christian spouse wherever possible.

The overall teaching of Paul in the New Testament is for Christians to marry fellow-Christians (2 Cor. 6:14 ff.). Why? Because light and darkness can't live together! Peter too assumes this to be the norm (verse 1). The reasons are fairly obvious: if marriage involves pulling together, how can this be achieved if the two partners are facing in different directions? Also, what if children come along? The dilemma increases.

This should be an encouragement to those who are single and thinking about marriage in future, to trust God from the start by limiting your choice of marriage partner to a Christian. And for those already married to non-Christians? All is not lost! Your partner may be won by your lifestyle (3:1–2).

Wives' submission

Is Peter pulling women down here? No! Actually Hebrew, Greek and Roman law regarded them as the possessions of their husbands. Here they are acknowledged as people with real choices, for example, choosing to follow Christ when their husbands won't. They are not to 'give way to fear' (verse 6), that is be bullied by their husbands to be like other women ('Forget the religion!'). Christian women can stand on their own two feet. This was first-century women's liberation! For their part husbands had to treat their wives with respect (verse 7). For further study see Ephesians 5:22–33 and 1 Corinthians 7:1–5.

Submission doesn't mean:

- Wives being inferior to their husbands. Jesus submitted to God and yet claimed 'I and the Father are one' implying equality (Jn. 10:30).
- Christian wives submitting to all men: 'they were submissive to their *own* husbands' (verse 5 author's italics).

- Unquestioning obedience. Only Jesus Christ deserves this (1:2)!
- Wives being second-class spiritually: 'husbands ... wives ... as heirs' together and praying together (verse 7).

Submission does mean:

- The wife submitting to God first: in 'reverence' (verse 2) and with 'hope in God' (verse 5). Without this any kind of submission on the human level is impossible.
- The wife being 'submissive' (verses 1, 5) to her own husband: respecting him and following his lead. Here we need to grasp the difference in culture between Peter's day and ours. For example in society (2:13–17) and the workplace (2:18–20) there is greater scope for Christians to have their say in many cultures today. Authority is more shared and this will affect our approach to submission in marriage. It will probably mean a sense of 'charting a course' together, with the ultimate responsibility resting with the husband.
- The husband and wife both regarding one another as a 'partner' (verse 7). Christian husbands are to 'live *with*' their wives as spiritual heirs '*with*' them (verse 7 author's italics). The basis for this is the biblical teaching on men and women joining in marriage and becoming 'one flesh' (Gn. 2:24; cf Eph. 5:31). A proper understanding of the wife's submission will not obscure this vital truth of partnership.

22

1 Peter 3:3–6

Christians at home: beautiful wives

Real beauty is linked to our relationship with God. It is found primarily on the inside rather than the outside. The Old Testament is full of examples of this godly 'attractiveness'.

Peter has just recommended a lifestyle for Christian partners that should act like a magnet, drawing their marriage partners to Christ (verses 1–2). What will this look like? The apostle broadens the scope of the discussion by talking about two kinds of beauty, one that is lasting and the other that fades with time.

Fashion is big business in the world today. Advertising too has an interest in the way we look. A right concern for looking after our bodies is stressed. All this applies to men as much as women. Fashion knows no bounds, except one's budget! Christians are not immune to pressure in this area. How should they view 'beauty'? Here there is a vivid contrast between beauty viewed from the outside and the inside, between an attractiveness that fades and one that is 'unfading' (verse 4).

Superficial beauty   Superficial beauty focuses primarily on the outside – what we do with our bodies and how we make them more attractive: ornate hairdos, expensive jewellery, and clothes that were definitely not 'off the peg'. In practice, this probably referred to well-off women in Peter's day. The apostle's plea in verse 3 is not to encourage scruffiness as a mark of spirituality (the worst-dressed Christian being the most 'spiritual' ...). The issue is one of emphasis: What strikes you when you first meet Miss/Mrs. X? Is it her make-up or her personality? Practically then, Peter is not saying 'No' to all jewellery for women. He *is* discouraging Christian women from making it the main issue. There is also a challenge for Christian men here: Do they look at women through God's eyes or the world's? Are looks the most important thing or character?

True beauty   Beauty then should be primarily internal – although a 'gentle and quiet spirit' (verse 4) will be seen on the outside too. Hair eventually goes grey; jewellery tarnishes over time; even the colouring of our clothes fades. But this is an 'unfading beauty' (verse 4). It has staying-power! And the heart of it?

- A 'gentle spirit': the quality that refuses to fight back, but waits for God to judge in the end.
- A 'quiet spirit': this does not mean saying nothing, but refers to exhibiting a sense of calm and tranquility. Someone whose 'feathers are not easily ruffled'.

Unlike attractive clothing, which often impresses others, this beauty is valued by God himself (verse 4): it receives *his* tick of approval! It also has the potential to draw non-Christians to Christ (verses 1–2). In thinking of beauty, therefore, we should bear in mind that:

- God is positively concerned about the beauty of our inner personalities (1 Sa. 16:7).
- Our danger, even as Christians, is to spend too much of our time, money and attention on the way we look.
- Primary attention should be given to the development of an attractive Christian character, which pleases God and draws others to Christ.

Peter now returns to his main theme, that of a Christian wife's submission to her husband. For an example of this kind of attractive behaviour we need look no further than the Old Testament women. Others have trodden this path before! Example, of course, is vital in the church: older women teaching younger women (Tit. 2:3–5); and young men learning from their 'elders' (1Pet. 5:5).

The most striking thing about these women is not their drive for 'beauty' but their God-centredness. They know who they are trying to please. Naturally, this would generally have met with their husbands' approval too. They were women prepared to be different because they 'put their hope in God'. Not that this was a private affair between them and God – they put it into practice by submitting to their husbands. Neither were they perfect in any sense! Rather this was the overall pattern of their lives.

One individual highlighted is Abraham's wife Sarah (verse 6): her submissive attitude was shown in obedience. Following Abraham was no 'fair-weather' experience and often involved going with him into dangerous and unknown territory (Gn. 12:1, 5; 13:1). Sarah must have trusted her husband to follow his lead.

Submission though did not mean Abraham failing to listen to his wife's perspective (Gn. 21:12). From Sarah's angle too, it is highly questionable whether she should have 'fallen in line' on two occasions by agreeing with Abraham's half-truth that she was his sister (Gn. 20:12; cf Gn. 12:10–20; 20:1–18). Peter himself limits Christian wives following Sarah's example to doing 'what is right' (verse 6).

Sarah's example then involves wives following their husbands' lead, often 'through thick and thin', but occasionally putting their foot down when this entails disobeying God's clear commands. In calling Abraham 'master' (verse 6 cf Gn. 18:12) she was using a title widely used in the east, showing genuine respect, not the cringing attitude of a servant.

Peter concludes this section by describing women who follow Sarah's example as her 'daughters', provided they fulfil the conditions set out. This may only mean that they follow her in being like her as wives. However, it could refer to something deeper. Elsewhere the church is portrayed as Abraham's spiritual 'children' through faith in Christ (Gal. 3:7). So to be Sarah's 'daughter' may mean that one is an heir of the promises given to Abraham and her.

To sum up: the apostle finishes off his call to a beautiful, submissive lifestyle by directing our gaze to the Old Testament women generally and Sarah in particular. They are examples to us now. The Old Testament then, is relevant for us today (1:10–12): in it are concrete examples of how to apply biblical teaching – even in the family sphere.

Questions

1. How are you tempted to impress others outwardly? Are there specifically 'Christian' ways of doing this? How can you guard against this danger?

2. *How is God a part of our family lives? In what sense is the church a family? How can we better serve those in our fellowship living alone?*

3. *Why is fashion big business in many countries today? Is it necessarily a bad thing? How do advertisers encourage us to spend money on the way we look?*

23

1 Peter 3:7

Christians at home: considerate husbands

Husbands aren't left out by Peter! They are responsible for their own attitudes and actions toward their wives. The goal is a happy family life and a healthy spiritual life.

People reading verses 1–7 today could accuse Peter of being somewhat sexist. He has devoted six verses to wives and reserves only one at the end for husbands! Can this charge stand? Basically not, for two reasons. First his teaching in verses 1–6 has plenty of relevance to Christian men. Second the apostle may be redressing a balance – it was quite unusual to address wives at the start anyway. Overall, there are lasting principles here for Christians of both sexes: concerning evangelizing those close to us and responding to the fashion culture around us.

So, Peter doesn't let himself or other married Christian men 'off the hook'! Christian wives have been taught their responsibilities. What about their partners? Here the standard is high indeed: the husband is given the task of imitating the self-sacrificing love of Christ for the church (cf Eph. 5:25–33). Wives would have little problem in submitting to such a husband. Peter's emphasis in verse 7 majors on the considerate use of God-given leadership.

A husband's love Where a wife *is* submissive it could be possible for a Christian husband to abuse his position by being thoughtless and inconsiderate towards her, neglecting to think about and meet her needs. Peter guards against this by talking about 'consideration in action'. From personal observation, it is all too easy for Christian husbands to have their minds elsewhere (for example, at work) and show a lack of thought; *or* to care in their hearts but fail to translate that into action. Peter's instruction to husbands is to be genuine servants, intent on meeting their wives' needs. This requires a real degree of thought and a measure of down-to-earth practicality too. We saw earlier that the Christian wife's behaviour could draw her partner to Christ. In like manner, the husband's behaviour will give an unspoken message to the world: of a Saviour who gave himself sacrificially for the church.

Furthermore, this consideration will be found in the bedroom as well as elsewhere: the word Peter uses here for 'live' often has sexual overtones (when used elsewhere in the Greek translation of the Old Testament). Scripture is not prudish, and Paul too speaks about Christian partners meeting one another's needs sexually (1 Cor. 7:1–5). Thankfully the Bible is not as coy as we sometimes are! Consideration is to be demonstrated here too.

A husband's respect   Secondly, the Christian husband is to be characterized by respect for his wife (verse 7). Again, this is to be shown concretely. Respect is no good if it is confined to the mind and attitudes alone. However, it will not come out if it is not there in the first place!

In thinking about respect, Christian husbands must remember two things: one that distinguishes them from their wives; the other that shows their equality with their wives.

Differences   Within the partnership, the wife must be shown special consideration and respect because she is the 'weaker partner' (verse 7). Clearly, from the immediate context this has nothing to do with the spiritual area of life – both husband and wife share jointly in God's salvation (verse 7). The term 'weaker partner' then, probably refers to the physical area of life.

Many people feel that women are physically less strong than men. Biological evidence would suggest, for example, that men have a greater muscle mass than women. Nonetheless in many parts of the world today women are involved in heavy manual labour and often have the strenuous task of bringing up children on their own. So what is Peter saying here about the wife as 'the weaker partner'?

His main point seems to be this: a husband (even a Christian one) could misuse his superior physical strength by, for instance, being violent in the house or abusing his wife sexually. This may be a particular temptation for non-Christian husbands (verses 1–2) who feel resentful about their wives' faith. Christian husbands too are warned not to be 'harsh' (Col 3:19) with their wives.

So, more broadly, the New Testament message is clear: the greater the apparent 'weakness' the *greater* the respect and consideration to be shown (cf 1 Cor. 12:22–24).

Similarities Differences, though, can be over-emphasised. Peter goes on to state the fact that spiritually, husband and wife are equal – alongside one another. As some translations put it, they are 'joint-heirs': rather like a married couple share a bank account which is in both their names and to which both have equal access! Christian marriage partners share equally in the gift they have received from God *and* the prayers they offer to God. Christian wives should never be treated as second-class citizens. Certainly the ministry of Jesus elevated women spiritually, when understood against the backcloth of contemporary Jewish ideas. The message then is 'Don't put the wrong emphasis on the differences between you. Do be sensitive to them, though.' Highlight your spiritual oneness in Christ: both in attitudes and actions.

Finally, living in this way will ensure that the husband's 'prayers' will not be hindered (verse 7). This could mean publicly at church; privately on his own; or together with his wife. Whatever the situation the motto is: 'Unloving attitudes and actions can seriously damage your spiritual health'. Sin not dealt with in the home will cause our prayers to bounce back off the ceiling.

Questions

1. *Peter seems to outline differences between men and women. What has 'feminism' done to ensure these differences are not over-emphasized? Why are there pitfalls in treating men and women as exactly the same?*

2. *Why should your church encourage healthy family life? How can this occur when Christians are often so busy? What is the link between unanswered prayer and family life?*

> 3. *Why do husbands and wives have different responsibilities? Is there any reason for Peter highlighting 'consideration' and 'respect' from husbands to their wives? How will consideration be shown in the sexual realm?*

Spiritual equality for husbands and wives

Despite physical differences, husbands and wives are spiritually equal. This doesn't mean that physical differences of gender are 'blotted out' in Christ but that in the spiritual realm God does not distinguish between men and women (cf Gal. 3:28). Men and women *together* form God's 'holy priesthood' (2:5).

By creation men and women together were made in the image of God, equal but different (Gn. 1:27, 5:1–2). In Christ they are spiritually 'on a par'. On the church's 'birthday' God's Spirit was poured out on 'both men and women' (Acts 2:18 cf Joel 2:29). When Paul taught about the Christian's 'sonship' he was using the word in the generic sense, referring to both male and female (Gal. 3:26). He says that 'there is neither ... male nor female, for you are all one in Christ Jesus' (Gal. 3:28). Two of Paul's closest colleagues were Priscilla and Aquila, a couple who ministered together spiritually (Acts 18:24–26).

Two qualifications need to be made:

1. Salvation doesn't make gender completely irrelevant – this appears to be Paul's teaching in the difficult passage on head-coverings (1 Cor. 11:2–16). Men and women must not totally forget their differences when praising God together. Paul's slogan could have been 'No unisex in worship!'
2. Salvation doesn't mean precisely the same responsibilities for husband and wife in Christian marriage: for example, according to Paul husbands have the greater responsibility of *loving* their wives, following Jesus' pattern of self-sacrifice (Eph. 5:22–23, 28, 33a). Wives for their part are to submit out of *respect* for their husbands (Eph. 5:22–23, 33b).

Practically this spiritual equality will mean, for example, the husband and wife taking each other's spiritual insights seriously and praying together too.

A POSITIVE APPROACH
TO WITNESSING
1 Peter 3:8–17

24

1 Peter 3:8–12

Pursuing peace – with insiders and outsiders

Our Christian calling is to bless believers and non-believers alike. This will result in us being blessed by God 'here and now'. To be blessed requires obedience on our part.

Peter is speaking about life within the Christian family, both in individual families (verses 1–7) and now in the wider family of the church (verse 8). In verses 9 onwards he moves from inside the individual and church family to outside: from relating to fellow-Christians to interfacing with the world at large. From 2:13 to 3:7 he has focused on specific groups of Christians (for example, slaves, wives, husbands) but now he turns to address 'all of you' (verse 8). There are no exemptions here. And a 'finally' (verse 8) halfway through the letter!

How then should we live: with each other and with a sometimes unfriendly world? By *being* a blessing to our fellow-Christians (verse 8) and *giving* a blessing to our non-Christian neighbours (verse 9).

Inside the 'family'   Life within the Christian family involves five things: First, we are to 'live in harmony with one another' (verse 8) sharing the same thoughts and attitudes without becoming 'clones'. Thus we are to take others into consideration, for example, when making decisions. And in an age of selfish individualism we are to avoid slipping into a 'survival of the fittest' mentality in the church.

Second, our emotions are to be involved too: our calling is to 'be sympathetic' towards each other (verse 8). We are to enter into the feelings of others as far as we are able and to do something about it when we can. In this we emulate the Lord Jesus who can sympathize with *us* in our weakness (Heb. 4:15).

Third, family love crops up a further time (cf 1:22; 2:17): we are to love other Christians as brothers (verse 8). This sensitivity to one another's thoughts and feelings should be a family quality! In a healthy family love will mean that conflict is tackled graciously when it occurs.

Fourth, Christians are to 'be compassionate' (verse 8). Compassion is vital for Christians attempting to minister to fellow-Christians who are experiencing difficulties. It can be described in this way: 'Everything within me went out to him/her'. This quality is particularly important in a society where we are so bombarded with needs that we can become cold and unfeeling and where so many people feel alienated and lonely.

Fifth, Christians are called to be humble (verse 8): the humility so despised by the Greeks was to be prized by Christians (cf 5:6). This does not mean 'putting ourselves down' but rather it is a willingness to take second place and put others first. It is a positive quality rather than a negative one.

The outcome of this kind of lifestyle will be the church as a harmonious 'symphony of grace': with fewer and fewer dud notes spoiling the music! Living with Christians, though, is not always heaven on earth and brings all manner of problems which need to be dealt with, but then, neither is interacting with a hostile world.

Outside the 'family'   What about our reactions to non-believers? How do we get on when evil is done to us or insults are thrown at us (verse 9)? The temptation to 'get even' may be much greater with those *outside* the family. Peter's answer is direct and simple: non-retaliation is the order of the day (verse 9)! Climbing into the ring is 'out'.

Nonetheless, we are not to be like sponges, simply absorbing evil and insults. We are to take the initiative by overcoming evil with good (cf Rom. 12:21) and positively 'blessing' others (verse 9). This doesn't refer to a pious 'God bless you!'. It actually means offering the gospel, with its promised blessings, to those currently eaten up with bitterness towards us. We are to respond graciously rather than act vehemently! The crucial test is this: will this situation control me, dragging me into 'getting even'? Or will I let Jesus be in control of it, by giving blessing in return? The first admits defeat from square one; the second is true victory. 'Don't let evil set the agenda!'

Why should we live this way? Not for purely human reasons, that is, for our good or the good of others, although these are relevant. Primarily it is because God's calling for his children is to 'inherit a blessing' (verse 9). Here Peter argues from the Old Testament again, using Psalm 34:12–16 as a carrot rather than a stick! Instead of using Scripture to beat us into submission, he quotes it to encourage us by showing what God has on offer: 'blessing ... life ... good days' (verses 9–10) and God's attention (verse 12a), but only if we fulfil the conditions of verses 10b–11!

On offer is 'good days'. This is not the promise of an easy life. Far from it! Psalm 34:19 anticipates 'many troubles' for the righteous. However, neither does Peter relegate God's blessing wholly to the future; there are blessings *now*! And he is certainly not teaching 'salvation by works' ('Live like this and God will bless you'). His readers have received salvation and so are within the family already.

Humanly, God promises a love of life (verse 10a): this is not something dependent on circumstances, otherwise Peter's suffering readers would not have qualified. Today, too, Christians living in tough situations of poverty or persecution can know this joy. Spiritually God promises the benefits of his own personal attention (verse 12a). There is a catch though, and it is not in the small print: the blessings on offer are for those willing to obey God in lips and lives. It is not a 'carte-blanche' promise. But what an incentive to know God's blessings here and now!

Questions

1. When did you last attempt to 'get even' with someone? How did you feel? What was your reaction? How does it compare with verse 9?

2. What are the current 'harmony levels' like in your church family (verse 8)? Why is our speech so important? How can you play your part in improving the quality of fellowship?

3. What evidence of 'tit for tat' (verse 9a) do you see between nations today (for example in the military realm; 'propaganda war')? Why is this so dangerous? How can Christians lead the way in responding properly to evil?

Use of the tongue

Here Peter seems to emphasize our speech as Christians: negatively in terms of avoiding insult (verse 9), evil and deceit (verse 10); positively in terms of prayer (verse 12). In his letter he gives further examples of the use of the tongue.

Jesus He was the only person not to commit any sin in his speech, that is, he told no lies (2:22 quoting Is. 53:9) and neither did he trade insult with insult (2:23).

His speech is a 'model' for us to follow (compare 2:22 and 3:10; and 2:23 and 3:9).

Christians Their speech is to be positive always: in prayer (1:17); in witness (3:15); in worship (2:9); and in the use of speaking gifts (4:11). Conversely believers are also warned against being interfering 'meddlers' (4:15) – the negative side of speech.

Non-Christians Verbal 'flak' or adverse criticism is a key strategy of theirs. Christians are accused of both doing wrong (2:12) and doing good (3:16)! Unbelievers' words are described as: accusation (2:12), abuse (4:4), and insult (4:14). Peter evaluates this speech as ignorant (2:15) and malicious (3:16) and says we receive it first and foremost because of our allegiance to Christ.

For further study of this theme the Old Testament 'wisdom literature' is very helpful. It speaks of the tongue being used for evil (Ps. 5:9; 34:13; 39:1; 52:4; Pr. 6:17; 17:20; 26:28; 28:23) or for good (Pss. 37:30; 51:14; 71:24; 119:172; Pr. 12:18). Essentially our tongue is to be controlled (Pr. 10:19; 21:23 cf Jas. 3:1–12). At root though, people's speech is a reflection of the state of their hearts according to Jesus (Lk. 6:45).

25

1 Peter 3:13–17

Doing good – whatever

Often the response to our lifestyle will be positive. Sometimes it will be hostile. When this happens don't give in to fear or silence. Keep honouring Christ in your heart and life!

Tennis players often play better when the crowd is on their side. If the spectators turn and support the person on the other side of the net their game can tend to suffer. Although we are not playing at our Christianity, what is the response to our lifestyle from those watching us?

God's response is clear: while he adamantly turns away from those doing evil, his gaze is firmly fixed on the righteous (verse 12). And the feedback from our fellow-Christians? Although not stated specifically, who wouldn't warm to the kind of family atmosphere described in verse 8? It is the type of church anyone would want to belong to! But what about onlookers and our consciences too?

Notice though the assumption made by Peter in verse 13: Christians generally are living the good life: they are eager to do what is 'good' and 'right' (verse 13); their behaviour is 'good behaviour' (verse 16), and any suffering they encounter is 'for doing good' (verse 17). So what is the response?

Crowd around In general, the response is best when Christians live as they should. Peter asks a rhetorical question in verse 13: 'Who is going to harm you if you are eager to do good?' The implied answer is

'No one!' The outsider to the church will on occasions applaud believers living for Christ: perhaps seeing an individual Christian's example; or viewing social work done by, say, the Salvation Army.

The reason for this is that non-Christians are not as unprincipled as we may sometimes imagine. In many areas they embrace high standards of morality and affirm others who do so because they too are made in God's image and likeness. Although fallen human beings like us, there is still a reflection of God seen in their response to what is good. But that is not the whole story!

Despite this general principle, the reality is often quite different. Christians can and do suffer for what is right and good (verses 14, 16). Like Peter's readers, they suffer abuse for not 'joining in' with pagan living (4:3–4), perhaps being described as adult 'goody-goodies' or 'holier than thou'. Worse still, Christian believers in Rome were soon to experience outright and violent persecution, as many of our fellow-Christians encounter in different parts of the world today.

Returning to our image of the tennis match, what is Peter's advice when the crowd is *not* on our side? It seems to be: 'Applause is OK. But keep playing well even when they're booing!' Why? – because the most important 'eyes' on you are God's (verse 12). He will carry on blessing you for doing right (verse 14a) even if they don't.

Conscience within   It is not only the crowd around who are watching though. The Christian's 'good life' is being monitored from within by his conscience (verse 16). Godly behaviour means keeping a good conscience. To use the example of a tennis match again: when we live God's way the 'moral umpire' inside says: 'It's good'. Your conscience is 'clear' (verse 16). However, a Christian with a muddied conscience, and 'out of sorts with God' may find the good life of fellow-Christians a real threat!

When under fire from non-Christians for living for God what should we do? Do we give in to fear? Peter goes to the heart of the matter in verses 14–15a. There are two alternatives when faced with suffering and the fear that goes with it. One is to give in to it; the other to replace it with Christ's kingly presence. The first option is illustrated in Isaiah 8:12 which describes Israel being threatened by Assyria and tempted to give in to intimidation (Is. 8:12). The antidote is to fear the Lord Almighty (Is. 8:13). Then God promises his people will be secure and their enemies will fall (Is. 8:14–15). The relevance to us is obvious: when we are under siege who are we most conscious of, the opposition or the Lord? And the Lord for Peter is 'Christ' (verse 15), a clear indication of the full deity of Jesus. So, what or who is occupying the central place deep inside us? Is fear my Lord, or is Christ? This needs to be firmly settled before anything else.

Do we give out our hope (verse 15)? Here the apostle emphasizes our readiness to explain our faith. We are not only to reject the way of fear in our hearts, but also the way of silence on our lips! Both can be a temptation when we are suffering for Christ. Instead of fighting back with insults (verse 9) the Christian is to be prepared to witness, answering questions provoked by a Christian lifestyle!

Our message then is one of 'hope' through Jesus (cf 1:3), a reality that is in short supply in our generation. It is also a reasonable message that makes sense. Our faith can be explained clearly even if we don't have *all* the answers to all the questions. We should be prepared for the common questions asked of our faith and have a reply ready. *How* we respond though is as important as what we say: answering questions with 'gentleness and respect' (verse 15). For example, we are not to make people appear idiotic for asking such things nor force our faith upon people. In short, there is nothing like a few questions to keep Christians 'on their toes'!

Finally then, what is the bottom line when suffering? Peter states that it is God's will that we keep on doing good regardless (verse 17 cf 4:19). That will embarrass the opposition (verse 16b).

Questions

1. *What questions are you most regularly asked by non-Christians? Which are the toughest to answer? As a witness, do you err in being too intellectual or too simple? Where is the balance?*

2. *Peter regularly mentions good behaviour. Why is it 'in Christ' (verse 16)? What does this phrase mean? How should our Christian living differ from being on our best behaviour? Does it?*

3. *Does the average person in your culture applaud Christians and their values or not? What are Christians doing together nationally to stand up for God's standards? How can we best support them?*

Giving an answer

The original Greek word for 'give an answer' is *apologia*. It has the sense of a defence lawyer speaking on his client's behalf. From this word we get the term 'apologetics' which is used to refer to the way Christians handle questions and defend their faith.

Paul saw this as central to his ministry. Frequently he defended both himself and his gospel (2 Tim. 4:16; Phil. 1:7, 16).

A good example of 'apologetics' is found in Acts 26. Paul has been accused by the Jewish authorities and this chapter records how he takes the initiative to defend himself and his gospel before the Roman authorities. His defence included:

- personal testimony (Acts 26:4–21)
- fulfilled prophecy (Acts 26:22–23)
- resurrection evidence (Acts 26:23, 26).

In this way he attempted to show that the gospel is 'true and reasonable' (Acts 26:25). We may be in a different setting, but the same task is ours.

Peter in his letter hints at two *kinds* of issues that may need tackling: the questions 'Is it true?' (for example, the resurrection of Jesus: 1:3 etc.) and 'Does Christianity work?' (for example, in the work place: 2:18–20).

THE HEART OF THE GOSPEL
1 Peter 3:18 – 4:6

26

1 Peter 3:18–20

Heart of the gospel

Jesus' death and resurrection are central to the gospel. God patiently waits for people to respond to this message. Regardless of numbers, they will be saved if they do so.

Again the theme of suffering draws Peter back to the heart of the good news: 'Christ died for sins' (verse 18: cf 2:24). These verses are sandwiched between his emphasis on our suffering as Christians (3:8–17 and 4:1). The key difference between here and 1 Peter 2:24 is that he doesn't stop at Jesus' crucifixion! Christ was 'made alive by the Spirit' (verse 18) and subsequently ascended and returned to the Father (verse 22). The overall feel is triumph following suffering!

First, 'Christ died for our sins'. Christ's death was a genuine historical event, recorded not only in the Bible but also in a number of other sources independent from the Bible. It happened 'in the body': that is, he died physically like any other human being (cf 2:24). Some try to deny this: for example, they say that Jesus *was* there but merely 'appeared to die'; or, according to many Muslims, he was replaced by a substitute. But the gospel record is clear – he *really* died! Even Pilate checked that the facts were true (Mk. 15:42–45). With the facts, too, comes the God-given meaning for us. This is no mere historical reporting, but includes the publisher's 'editorial' comment too! Jesus' death dealt with the distance between us and God. He died 'to bring you to God' (verse 18).

Second, this was a 'once for all' act (cf Heb 9:26; 10:10). The sacrifices under the old agreement between God and Israel went on and on: they had to be continually repeated to deal with sins. The end result was to continually remind people of their failures (Heb. 10:3) which was not good news. But the cross is a reminder of sins *forgiven* and in taking communion this 'once for all' act of forgiveness and mercy is brought to our attention again and again (1 Cor. 11:24–25).

So the death of Jesus on the cross really happened! It really matters! Why? Because on the cross an exchange took place: Jesus bore the punishment for our sins in exchange for us receiving his righteousness. In stamp collecting I used to exchange duplicate stamps for others I hadn't got. Both my friends and I benefited. Here though, Jesus willingly took the raw end of the deal: he took the punishment for our 'unrighteous' living (verse 18). Effectively, he was 'distanced' from the Father (Mt. 27:46) so that we could be brought near to him. It was the most staggering 'swap' in history: humanly 'unfair' but divinely gracious!

Death is not the terminus though: resurrection follows. Here Peter draws a contrast between 'body' and 'Spirit' (verse 18). This does not refer to different aspects of Christ's person (that is, his humanity and divinity), but rather, the apostle is speaking about different phases of his experience: on the human plane he genuinely died; on the spiritual plane he is truly alive (in bodily resurrected form of course!). Peter uses a similar contrast in his Pentecost sermon: 'You ... put him to death ... But God raised him from the dead' (Acts 2:23–24). God's 'but' wins the day! The world's mistaken verdict on Jesus is overturned and Jesus is raised by the power of the Holy Spirit (cf Rom. 8:11).

We come now to two verses (verses 19–20) that scholars have wrestled hard with through the ages. What is happening here and why the link with Noah's day (cf Gn. 6 – 8)? In passing, it is worth noting that these verses, together with 4:6, are sometimes used to argue for 'a second chance to repent after death' (See *Second chance after death*). Three questions arise from this section:

- Who are the 'spirits' being preached to?
- When did the preaching occur?
- What was the message preached?

There are endless speculations on these questions but two main explanations are possible:

First the 'spirits' could be disobedient demons (as opposed to angels on God's side). Christ preaches to them after his death, or probably following his resurrection, his message being to confirm his victory over them through the cross (Col. 2:15). They are both defeated and 'in submission' to him (verse 22).

Second the 'spirits' could be disobedient people living in Noah's day. Christ, by the Spirit, preaches to them through Noah, giving them a chance to repent before the flood comes. (NB: See *Jesus' preaching to 'Spirits'* to assess these approaches.)

What can we learn from these two possible options? Applying the first explanation to our situations we, like Peter's readers, suffer for our faith on occasions. Behind this suffering ultimately lies 'our enemy the devil' (5:8) and his demons. We need to be aware that through Christ's death the opposition from the devil is *defeated*. This was underlined by Christ personally (verse 19). His enemies are currently 'in submission' to him (verse 22). Instead of suffering in a resigned way we can press on with a sense of triumph. Final and complete victory is on its way!

Applying the second explanation we, like Noah, should be bold and forthright in our witness (cf 3:15). Although we are in a minority, as he and his family were, we too will be saved and final judgment will come as surely as the flood did (cf 2 Pet. 3:6–7). It is an encouragement to know that all evil will be dealt with then, including that of our persecutors (2 Thess. 1:5–10)!

Finally, two 'spurs' to our witness can be learnt from the flood-event: God 'waited patiently' (verse 20) during the building of the ark. This 'patience' means there was a chance for repentance and salvation (cf 2 Pet. 3:9, 15). Despite the evil of Noah's day, God's grace was offered. He is still waiting today!

'A few people' were saved in Noah's day (verse 20) which was a big encouragement for Peter's readers as a scattered, lonely minority. It is a boost also to Christians today in countries where the church is small as a proportion of the population: Keep going!

Questions

1. *Why is understanding the phrase 'once for all' (verse 18) important for your Christian life? Do you try to add to what Christ has done in some way? How?*

2. *How effective is your church in preaching to 'outsiders'? What is the response like (for example compared to Noah's day)? How is Noah a good example of being a 'fool for Christ' (1 Cor. 4:10)?*

> 3. *In which parts of the world today is the church a small minority? What is the 'majority faith' in these countries? How can we encourage our fellow-Christians there both practically and in prayer?*

Jesus' preaching to 'spirits'?

To assess the two possible explanations to verse 19 above, it must be said that 'spirit' can refer to angelic beings (good or bad) *or* human beings (compare the way Peter uses 'your soul' in 2:10 to mean 'you as a person viewed from a spiritual angle'. This alone won't decide which explanation is correct! The problems with each are:

The first explanation This poses an important question: what is the connection between the demons preached to after Jesus' death (or resurrection) and Noah's day? The usual answer is that they were the 'sons of God' who lived before the time of Noah (Gn. 6:2, 4). In the book of 1 Enoch in the Apocrypha they are described in detail, for example their detention 'in prison' for disobedience (cf 2 Pet. 2:4–5; Jude 6). However, the biblical record stresses human sin rather than the sin of demons calling forth God's judgment (Gn. 6:5–13).

The second explanation The main problem here is how could Christ speak through Noah? Some argue for a parallel with Old Testament prophets (1:10–12) where the 'Spirit of Christ' spoke through them. Why can't Christ, by his Spirit, speak through Noah? A second difficulty is of these people being 'in prison'. When is this referring to? – in Christ's day or Noah's?

On balance the first explanation seems more likely.

27

1 Peter 3:20–22

Response to the gospel

Baptism is vitally important. It marks the outward beginning of our Christian lives. To be real though, it must be linked to an inner 'bath' and a genuinely risen Jesus.

Eight people in the ark were 'saved through water' (verse 20). Water was the means of salvation (bearing up the ark) and the means of judgment (drowning the disobedient). For Peter though, it is more than that: it is a picture of Christian baptism. And this baptism 'saves you' (verse 21)! What does the apostle mean?

First Peter draws a parallel between the people and events of Noah's day and those of his own. This comes out in the word 'symbolises' (literally meaning 'antitype' – that which corresponds to). So baptism corresponds in some way to salvation through water at the time of Noah. We must be careful of seeing too close a parallel though: Noah's family were saved by avoiding the water while for Peter's readers salvation was linked to getting into it! The important point is the connection between water and salvation in both cases.

However, Peter *does* say that 'baptism ... now saves you'. Some today take this to mean that going through the motions of being baptized (whether as an adult or an infant) produces automatic salvation: a view often called 'baptismal regeneration'. This is in conflict with the New Testament emphasis on salvation by faith in Jesus (Eph. 2:8). Peter himself identifies Christians as those who have faith in God (1:21) and believe in Christ (2:7). By contrast, non-Christians 'do not believe' (2:7; 3:1).

Our initial response must be to say that in New Testament times baptism was an important part of the 'salvation package'. It was the basic way faith was openly exhibited (Acts 2:38). However, Peter helps us here by outlining what he does and doesn't mean about baptism.

He doesn't mean baptism is 'the removal of dirt from the body' (verse 21). It has little correspondence with having a shower after a gruelling day in the garden. Rather, it represents an *inner* cleansing or washing. Peter himself was assured that he had already had a complete 'bath' spiritually (Jn. 13:10). He was clean. We are too! This phrase also guards us from thinking that the water itself has magical cleansing qualities – rather like one of today's sophisticated washing powders ('One wash and completely free of stains'!). Baptism then symbolizes a thorough, lasting wash inside.

He does mean that baptism is 'the pledge of a good conscience toward God' (verse 21). Without this it is just a ritual and cannot be properly said to be baptism. The term 'pledge' can be understood in two ways:

- a *request* made to God for a clear conscience on the basis of Christ's work for us
- a *promise* to keep a clear conscience, with his help, from baptism onwards (probably made by candidates in response to questions asked at the time of baptism).

Both would seem appropriate to the beginning of the Christian life. The first seems more likely in context. Practically then, baptism is a 'marker' for us: of the time we asked for forgiveness and cleansing; and of the occasion we committed ourselves to live for him.

So, baptism cannot be divorced from our inner experience. Neither can it be separated from the historical facts about Christ. Thus 'it saves you by the resurrection of Jesus Christ' (verse 21). Baptism then has no real significance if it is not vitally linked to faith in the biblical Christ. Why? Because it vividly pictures his death, burial and resurrection (Rom. 6:1–14) and our oneness with him in those events!

There are two vital questions then, to ask about baptism:

- Does it represent an inner cleansing that has already taken place?
- Is that cleansing a direct result of what Jesus has done for us in his death and resurrection?

Peter now moves towards a 'mini-creed' or statement of Christian belief. Having spoken of Jesus' death (verse 18) and resurrection (verses 18, 21) he goes on to talk of what followed. Forty days after his resurrection, Jesus ascended to the Father (Acts 1:9–11). Here he was given the ultimate position of power and authority which is symbolized by being given the seat of honour at God's right hand (cf Heb. 1:3). Crucifixion, resurrection, ascension, coronation! And the significance of where he is now? He is reigning! He was lower than the angels for a short while (Heb. 2:7) but is now actively ruling over 'angels, authorities and powers'. For Peter's readers this will not produce a rebellious attitude to earthly authorities (2:13–17). It will encourage them, though, to realize that hostile spiritual authorities are now under Jesus' control. Even the 'roaring lion' (5:8) is resistible.

In summary then, salvation is by faith. Such faith is normally expressed by being baptized. But for baptism to be genuine it must be linked to two things: firstly to our individual experience – an inner cleansing through Jesus' blood; secondly, 'outside' our experience – the historical event of Jesus' resurrection (bringing us new life).

Questions

1. *What does it mean to have 'a good conscience' as a Christian? How can you maintain it? What steps should you take if you experience a bad conscience?*

2. *Where does your church stand on the issue of baptism? Do you understand its teaching? Have you expressed your faith in this way (or an 'equivalent' way in your tradition)?*

3. *What are the 'angels, authorities and powers' over which Jesus reigns? Do you think they have any influence on human power structures? How? Why is this good news for those who feel powerless living under evil régimes?*

Baptism

'Baptisms' are part of the basics for Christian living (Heb. 6:2). The New Testament describes two types of baptism: in the Holy Spirit (for example, Mt. 3:11b; 1 Cor. 12:13); in water (for example, Mt. 3:11a; Acts 2:38, etc.). Both speak of Christian beginnings. Here in 1 Peter the context indicates baptism in water.

In the first century, baptism was one part of responding to the gospel (repentance; faith; baptism; receiving the Spirit) and was considered to be the norm for demonstrating Christian faith (Acts 2:38). Examples of baptism by water are found in:

- the Gospels   Jesus was baptized (Mt. 3:13–17) and taught that new disciples should be too (Mt. 28:19).
- Acts   The early church included baptism in their gospel presentation (Acts 2:38; 8:35–38) and practised it (for example, Acts 16:31–33).
- Letters   Paul and others *assumed* their readers were baptized – having expressed their oneness with Jesus (for example, Rom. 6:1–14).

Most Christians today agree on the importance of baptism in the name of the Father, Son and Holy Spirit, the exception being those who downplay the importance of outward symbols. Bible-believing Christians though, differ on two questions:

- When?   Should babies be baptized in prayerful hope of coming to faith later on; *or* believing adults (and children) be baptized following personal confession of faith?
- How?   Should a small amount of water be sprinkled on babies *or* believing adults (and children) be put completely under the water?

Understanding Jesus being 'glorified'

All the important events about Jesus are found in 1 Peter: from his birth ('revealed': 1:20) to his second coming ('revealed': 1:7,13, etc.). Here Peter describes 'the glories that would follow' Christ's sufferings and death (1:11) including his:

Resurrection   Jesus was raised 'from the dead' (1:3, 21), and 'made alive by the Spirit' (3:18). The resurrection is vital for our initial believing (1:21) and our present hoping (1:3). The fact of him being alive now is assumed throughout the letter: for example, our sacrifices and praises reach God through him (2:5; 4:11). The resurrection is particularly relevant for Christians suffering bereavement (see comments on 4:6): physical death was not the end for Christ (3:18) – it is not for believers either.

Ascension   This is only briefly referred to here in 1 Peter. The importance of the ascension is explained elsewhere in the New Testament: Jesus' going away is for our good, because it means the sending of the

Spirit, 'the Counsellor' (Jn. 16:7 etc.). The Spirit's ministry is essential for our Christian living and witness (1:2–12).

Coronation   Jesus is at 'God's right hand', ruling the spiritual powers (verse 22) that lie behind the opposition Peter's readers were experiencing. In Christ we too are spiritually raised and seated '... with him in the heavenly realms ...' (Eph. 2:6). This truth lies behind the victory in spiritual warfare promised in 5:8. Jesus' coronation is also important because he is continuously praying for us (Heb. 7:25) and speaking to God on our behalf: 'in our defence' (1 Jn. 2:1).

28

1 Peter 4:1–3

'Us': living for God's will

Jesus' clear-cut attitude to sin is our 'model'. And time too is moving on. Let us determine to leave sin behind and press on into God's will.

At first glance these verses are a 'minefield', especially verse 1! Let us clear some of the 'mines' to start with. These verses raise the following questions:

1. What does it mean to have the same attitude as Christ in our suffering (verse 1)? Does this mean our suffering has direct benefit for others (cf 2:24; 3:18)? Of course not! It can have benefit for *us* though (verse 2).
2. Is the body the cause of our problems (verse 1)? The impression could be gained that inflicting suffering on our bodies will make us more holy. This is not correct (cf Col. 2:20–23).
3. Are Christians who suffer the most the least sinful? Not necessarily! For those who respond badly to suffering it can be a 'downhill experience'. Suffering can cause us to give up the fight against sin.
4. Does 'done with sin' (verse 1) mean we will have no further problems with it for the rest of our lives? Unfortunately not: the 'war' continues (2:11)! Even Christians committed to obedience need fresh cleansing on occasions (1:2).

So what is Peter saying?

In returning again to Christ's sufferings, he is drawing attention to the *kind* of suffering he experienced. It was the suffering of a righteous person (3:18). Ours is to be for the same reason (3:14). Also, his death marked a 'cut-off point' for sin (3:18 cf 2:24). Peter mentions the body of Jesus twice, telling us that this suffering really happened physically; it was not like an unreal nightmare! Also, it reminds us that sin can take place in real 'flesh and blood' human beings like us.

How then can we arm ourselves with Jesus' attitude? We need to say a firm 'Good-bye' to sin and a warm 'Hello' to God's will! There is a 'war' on (2:11) and it involves not giving in to sinful desires. No one with any sense enjoys a battle for the sake of it. Rather they want to make sure it is engaged in for right reasons. Jesus fought the battle on the cross to give us a decisive break with sin (2:24) although he, personally, needed no such break (2:22). Sharing his attitude then means treating sin as *past tense*. It is to be treated as a 'has-been' for the Christian! Our mind-set is to be enemies to sin and friends with righteousness, whatever the cost involved. This is to be the whole tenor of our lives.

Suffering challenges us with the question of whether or not we are willing to pay the price of doing God's will. The alternative is to cave in to sin and wave the white flag of surrender! But with the right kind of mental ammunition the result is this: suffering for what is right should strengthen our resolve to leave sin behind (verses 1-2). If we are willing to bear the cost of obeying God it shows we have already made up our minds that sin is dead and gone for us. It is not an option any more. Peter's argument here is similar to that of Paul in Romans 6:1-14: 'We died to sin; how can we live in it any longer?' (Rom. 6:2) and baptism is a picture of our oneness with Christ (Rom. 6:3).

Two steps are necessary for conquering sin:

- Firmly making up our minds that sin is 'past tense'.
- Underlining that decision when suffering for what is right by carrying on living properly regardless.

Thinking in this way will divide life into two parts for us: what is to come ('the rest of his earthly life': verse 2) and what has been ('time in the past': verse 3). Here Peter has a sense of the importance of time. Days, months and years are precious for the Christian. With sin 'enough is enough!' We've got a whole life ahead of us to live for God.

The future (verse 2) Our attitude to sin means that our choices are already made although in practice we have to go on living them out! Desires are not wrong in themselves but ours as believers should be directed to God's will which is our 'sanctification' (1 Thess. 4:3). Sanctification means being made holy so that in everyday life *his* desires increasingly become ours. And our prayer should be 'Your will be done, on earth as it is in heaven' (Mt. 6:10). Because of this mind-set Peter encourages us to make our decision in advance: 'No' to sin; 'Yes' to God's will.

The past (verse 3) Another argument for living this way is because we have already wasted some of our lives. Peter's readers could remember their past well enough. They had lunged into sin partly out of 'ignorance' of God (1:14)! Now they know better. The apostle highlights three areas of sin that are very relevant to our own day: sex; alcohol; idols (verse 3). Sex is good and God-given in marriage, but we are to run from immorality (1 Cor. 6:18). Drunkenness is off-limits for the Christian: there is a better way – Spirit-filled living (Eph. 5:18). And we are to keep ourselves from idols (1 Jn. 5:21). Idols are not only actual statues of gods but they can be anyone or anything that takes God's unique place in our lives, for example, money, possessions, other people.

So, in the light of Jesus' attitude to sin and our clear-cut attitude to it too, we are to turn away from sin and welcome God's will with enthusiasm (cf Rom. 13:11–14).

Questions

1. *Are you 'done with sin'? If not, what will help you make this vital decision? If you have, how can you stay that way?*

2. *What should we do to encourage one another in the war against sin? How can we encourage those in our fellowship paying a heavy price for doing God's will?*

3. *How accurately does verse 3 describe people in your culture? What is your verdict on how 'pagan' your society is? Where should we draw the line in our Christian involvement with others, for example, in the use of our leisure-time?*

Pagans

Peter mentions 'pagans' twice (2:12; 4:3): first to describe the people believers lived amongst and second to remind his readers of their 'pagan' lifestyle before becoming Christians.

In the New Testament the word 'pagan' (or similar) was used initially by Jews referring to non-Jews or Gentiles (Mt. 5:47; 18:17). Paul referred to non-Christians as pagans (1 Cor. 5:1) as did John (3 Jn. 7).

Finally Paul described the Corinthian Christians before their conversion as pagans (1 Cor. 12:2).

Some good things are said about 'pagans': they have a real sense of 'family loyalty' (Mt. 5:47) and some have higher moral standards than those found within the church (1 Cor. 5:1).

However, the pagans were condemned for idolizing material possessions (Mt. 6:32; Lk. 12:30) and worshipping idols and demons (1 Cor. 10:20; 12:2). Further, those that were religious were criticized by Jesus for believing that the volume of words spoken in prayer was the most important aspect (Mt. 6:7).

The Greek word *ethnos* refers to a large group of people with something in common. Our English word 'heathen' comes from this! In twentieth-century terms, a pagan usually refers to a person who has no religion or who disregards belief in God. 'Pagans' in first-century Asia Minor would probably have been characterized by a mixture of superstitious religion and low morals.

29

1 Peter 4:4–6

'Them': proceeding to God's judgment

Non-Christians are often shocked when we don't 'join in'! But we know that everyone will have to answer to God for their actions. Our Christian friends who are physically dead are spiritually alive now!

'Us and them': Peter has just addressed Christians ('you': verses 1–3), comparing their previous lifestyle with that of 'pagans' (verse 3). He now focuses on these pagans ('they': verses 4–5) and on those in the Christian family who have died ('they': verse 6).
Regarding pagans Peter talks about two forms of assessment: how pagans assess us (verse 4) and how God assesses them (verse 5).

'Pagans' have a habit of exchanging God for substitutes and 'living for kicks' (verse 3). Peter likens this to plunging into a 'flood' of dirty water! The word used here (verse 4) is of a wide stream or water poured out in power. Everything is carried along to the limit, to excess! The word translated as 'plunge' in verse 4 had the idea of 'running' in the original Greek: running headlong into the flood of evil. This is dissipation, a reckless drive for pleasure without any brakes put on, just as the prodigal son frittered away his father's wealth on his own pleasure and gratification (Lk. 15:13).

The surprise is that Christians who used to join in (verse 3) don't anymore. They have upset the boat altogether by their change of tack. The response of those around is confusion. They cannot grasp why we won't 'conform' (1:14) any more like everyone else. Our behaviour is a threat to them, because it challenges their standards and makes them wonder if they are in the wrong! Because they feel threatened, 'they heap abuse on you' (verse 4) and the Christian is treated as the odd one out. Peter's readers may have been viewed as bad citizens because they didn't join in the imperial cult (cf 2:13). The pagans' aim is to put pressure on us to return to their so-called normality but the apostle's advice is 'continue to do good' (4:19).

We do not toe the line so those around make us feel outsiders in a barrage of words. But theirs is not the final say. *God* has the last word! What he says at the end of the day is what really counts. His judgment is not optional, but compulsory. We have no choice as to whether we turn up for judgment or not. Further, it is coming soon: 'the end of all things is near' (verse 7). God is perfectly 'ready' for the day of judgment, despite what some think (2 Pet. 3:3–10). Finally, judgment is for everyone: it is comprehensive, covering 'the living and the dead' (verse 5). God is impartial in his judgment (1:17), and so no-one will be left out. Judgment involves giving an 'account' to God (verse 5) as our 'Creator' (verse 19). We are responsible to him for our lives. What have we done with his good gifts? Have we replaced him with other 'gods'? How have we treated his people (cf 2 Thess. 1:5–7)?

So: criticism is a present-tense experience for Christians; judgment is a future-tense experience for everyone. But, in the light of God judging even the 'dead' (verse 5), what about our Christian friends who have died already (cf 1 Thess. 4:13–5:11)? How about those we used to know who accepted the gospel during their lifetime?

Peter answers this (verse 6) by reminding his readers that the gospel they heard, and we heard, is only good news against the backcloth of bad news – God's judgment against sin (verse 5). However, this good news of 'grace' (5:12) was preached to *and* received by our Christian friends in their lifetime. They won't be deserted by the 'Shepherd' now.

This message is fine for believers, but the average non-Christian views all this as pie in the sky when you die: 'Your Christian friends die like everyone else. And I thought this was a resurrection-faith'! For many today death is the end of the road and any talk of an after-life is nonsense. They believe that 'When you die you rot, whatever your previous beliefs or behaviour'. Although these views are wrong, they can be disturbing for Christians, especially those worried about Christian friends or family now physically dead. Besides, what about *our* future too?

There are two quite different responses to this.

Humanly speaking We *are* physical people (in the 'body'). In this sense death is the terminus of the human body for all people, whether Christians or not. Nonbelievers will say this is the end of the story but for Christians it is only the beginning: life in the fullest sense, with a new body, really starts at death!

Spiritually speaking Physically dead Christians are now truly alive with God as they follow the 'pattern' of Jesus (3:18b), life following death.

So, there are two perspectives on death (verse 6): for the non-Christian it is a tragic end, but for the Christian a glorious beginning!

Nonetheless in their daily lives a lot is being thrown at Christians: they are often criticized for not joining in now, and their future hope is under attack too. In effect people are saying: 'There *shouldn't* be a difference between Christians and non-Christians, and there *won't* be!' Peter's response is that this is completely untrue! After God's judgment there is either spiritual life or spiritual death. Therefore it *does* matter how we live now. And even if we get 'persecuted' on earth for being Christians, we will know fullness of life in the future.

Questions

1. *Why is it important to preach the good news to people now? Is there anyone you know near to the end of their lives who you can befriend, pray for or witness to?*

2. *How is bereavement tackled in your fellowship? What is done for people losing Christian or non-Christian loved ones? Is there any way care could be improved?*

3. *What kind of threat is Christian living to people in your culture (cf verse 4)? Why is it not more so? How do non-Christians respond to the idea of justice? What differences are there between experiencing justice at the hand of a magistrate and facing God's judgment?*

'Second chance' after death

Some think the preaching mentioned in 1 Peter 3:19 and 4:6 refer to the same occurrence: people being given another chance after death to repent. This is doubtful. The word 'preached' in the NIV is a translation from two quite different Greek words: the first (3:19) is used of a proclamation, not always of welcome news! The second (4:6) is nearly always used of Christians preaching the *good* news of Jesus. If 3:19 (explained earlier) and 4:6 are not linked as seems likely, what does 4:6 and the rest of Scripture have to say about this idea of a second chance?

'The dead' (4:6) are obviously physically dead (cf verse 5). Were they preached to before or after death? (The word 'now' in verse 6 is not included in the original letter!) Peter stresses in 4:1–6 the importance of our behaviour now in the light of the coming judgment (verse 5). If there is a 'second chance' then why bother to say this? In fact, 4:6 probably parallels Paul's concerns in 1 Thessalonians 4:13ff in helping believers to cope with the pain of losing Christian friends.

The 'second chance' idea is foreign to 1 Peter. Peter emphasizes believing for those presently alive ('believers' – 2:17) and the finality of God's judgment (cf 4:5, 7).

A key verse in the New Testament is Hebrews 9:27: '... man is destined to die once, and after that to face judgment.' Jesus too taught that the 'great chasm' cannot be bridged after death (Lk. 16:19–31) and there is no second opportunity then (Mt. 25:1–13).

A POSITIVE APPROACH TO LIVING
1 Peter 4:7–19

30

1 Peter 4:7–9

'The end is nigh': Christian graces

When we realize that the end of the world is near and Jesus' return is imminent, it should spur us on to practical Christian living. Prayer, love and hospitality are vital ingredients.

'The end is nigh' proclaims the preacher. This is a biblical truth but often conveyed with a resigned kind of attitude and a pessimistic tone of voice. For Christian believers though, it is a statement of *triumph*, and one that radically affects our lives today.

For Peter's readers in Asia Minor, suffering for their faith, the 'end' was good news: of God visiting his people (2:12); of Jesus being revealed (1:7, 13); of an end to their suffering (5:10). Away with the doom-merchants! Fixing our attention on the end also produces action not inaction. Just as a family on the last day of their holiday are packed and ready to return home the next day, instead of passively waiting for tomorrow they make the very best of their final day. This is in stark contrast to some of the Thessalonian Christians, who packed in their jobs because of the nearness of Jesus' coming (cf 1 Thess. 5:1–3 and 2 Thess. 3:6–13). For us the fact that 'the end is nigh' should be a spur to developing the Christian graces of waiting, praying, loving and welcoming.

Waiting   What then is the 'end'? It is not of course, the end of God and his purposes: he has *endless* glory and power (verse 11)! Christians too are given 'eternal glory in Christ' (5:10). The original Greek word for 'end' means the goal towards which history is heading. We are not going round and round in endless circles: history is going somewhere and there is a terminus at the end of the road. To use the picture of athletics there is a finishing tape, and we are fast approaching the final straight: 'the end of all things is near' (verse 7). One main event is imminent in God's salvation timetable – the revelation of Jesus Christ (1:13).

Although Peter stated that the end was near it did not occur in Peter's day, and two thousand years later, it still has not. How do we respond? Jesus warned of such delay and how to cope with it (Mt. 24:45–51). Peter too explained the apparent 'hold-up' from our angle in terms of God waiting to give people a chance to change (2 Pet. 3:9). Our completed salvation is 'ready' to be revealed and God is 'ready' to judge the world (1:5; 4:5). In the meantime, every generation of Christians is to live as if it were the last, not with a sense of furious panic but rather expressing God's grace through our lives and ministries. Besides if we did know the precise date of the 'end' what difference would it make to those faithfully living out the Christian life?

Praying   Falling asleep in prayer (Mt. 26:40, 43, 45) had obviously contributed much to Peter's learning curve! He had grown through his mistakes and was able to teach others. His main message seems to be that prayer is not a form of escapism: a kind of 'head in the clouds' spirituality. In fact, we need to *keep* our heads! Peter's readers could have given in to fear or anxiety because of their neighbours' opposition with the result that they made decisions without thinking them through properly. Prayer, then, calls for us to be 'clear-minded' which is especially relevant in a day of 'information overload'!

Secondly, all our faculties need to be alert to pray: we are to be 'self-controlled' (literally 'sober'). Drunkenness of course, alters our perspective, slows us down, and has nasty after-effects. We find we can't function properly. Prayer, however, requires us to be fully alert in every way. We need to give God our best in terms of time and space. Prayer is not something to intoxicate us and give us an escape-route from the harsh realities of life.

These qualities are needed for the sake of 'your prayers': either our ongoing praying throughout the day as individuals *or* our corporate prayers together as a church family.

Loving   Loving is the next grace Peter highlights although it is the first priority 'above all ...' (verse 8). His stress on love (cf 1:22; 3:8) shows how much importance he attaches to real caring among Christians. Peter may have emphasized love because his persecuted readers were subject to a Satanic 'divide and conquer' strategy (cf Phil. 1:27–28). Genuine love, then, is paramount. Perhaps painful splits in churches today could sometimes be avoided through a *deeper* love. Deep-shaft mines in Britain produce good coal, but very expensively. Likewise Christian love costs if it is anywhere near real! It also covers sins (Pr. 10:12). This is no 'cover-up', pretending sin is not there, but more a forgiving of the sins of our fellow-Christians and not deliberately exposing their failures to public view. Love does not, however, exclude discipline being exercised in the case of Christians who have fallen badly morally and are unwilling to change their ways (1 Cor. 5:1–13). When they do repent though, our responsibility is to *reaffirm* our love for them (2 Cor. 2:5–11, especially verse 8).

Welcoming   Sometimes 'love' is too general a word. How does it work tangibly? One way is by welcoming our brothers and sisters with 'hospitality' (verse 9). This was crucial in the first century where inns were often centres of immorality, and where churches had no buildings to meet in. It is vital today too, for example putting people up for the weekend; opening your home regularly for a housegroup; showing hospitality to the elderly, people living on their own, and single parents. Whatever the amount of space available, an open heart will always find room!

However, this can sometimes take its toll on us: in time, energy, money, inconvenience. Thus Peter's 'rider' is that we are to be uncomplaining about welcoming others (verse 9) even if the dishes are left unwashed at the end of an evening! An acid-test of love is: are we really glad to open our homes to one another?

The 'end' then, will not lead to passive resignation for Christians, but rather to getting on with life, and to exercising the graces God gives us: waiting, praying, loving, and welcoming.

Questions

1. *What kinds of practical hindrances do you experience in prayer? How have you dealt with them? Why is focusing on 'the end' helpful in prayer?*

> 2. *Why does Peter emphasize hospitality? Is hospitality actively encouraged in your particular fellowship? How can it be improved: by your personal example, by better overall planning?*
>
> 3. *World-wide exposure has recently been given to sins of immorality and fraud among prominent Christian leaders. How will Christian love 'cover' these sins? In what ways shouldn't it?*

Loving one another

Peter reminds his readers to love one another on three occasions (1:22; 3:8; 4:7). He wasn't averse to 'reminders' (2 Pet. 1:12; 3:1)! What is this love like?

First, by nature it is high-priority and family-orientated. Peter's statement, 'Above all, love ...' (verse 8) puts a premium on such love, just as Jesus did (Jn. 13:34–35). He too *repeated* his new command: 'Love each other' (Jn. 15:12). Christian love is also primarily 'in-house'; that is, it is directed to fellow-Christians, and is part of being 'family' together (3:8). However, it is also directed to 'outsiders' (see 3:9). The word used twice in verse 8 (Greek *agape*) refers particularly to God's quality of self-sacrificing love.

Second, the quality of this love is to be deep and genuine: 'deeply, from the heart' (1:22). The word 'deep' actually pictures a horse at full-stretch, keeping going even when it is painful. Love is also to be sincere and from the heart. We are not actors 'playing at love': it must be real.

Third, the exercise of Christian love is to be forgiving and practical. It 'covers over a multitude of sins' (4:8) which refers to our love covering *other's* sins, rather than our love for others covering *our* sins! Practicality is also at the heart of mutual love (cf 1 Jn. 4:17–18), a good example being hospitality (verse 9).

31

1 Peter 4: 10–11

'The end is nigh': Christian gifts

For us and our churches, God's praise is paramount. A church fellowship that works together as a team will bring real glory to him. Each of us then should 'pull our weight' by using our gifts.

The final whistle is about to be blown. Five minutes of the match remain! Now is not the time for any player to flag. Everyone should play as a team into the dying seconds. 'The end of all things is near' (verse 7): therefore, we are to go 'all out' in practical Christian living *and* in using our God-given gifts too. Good teamwork depends on each person employing his or her respective skills and the same goes for the church. And the applause is directed to heaven rather than to the player on the field!

Looking at this paragraph as a whole (verses 7–11) it is worth noting the marvellous balance here between graces and gifts. Graces (verses 7–9) are those aspects of Christian living we are all called to display. Gifts (verses 10–11) are specific abilities given to individuals by the Holy Spirit to serve God and others. *All* Christians are to pray, love, and be hospitable. Thus when asked to put someone up for the night we can't reply 'It's not my gift!'. Conversely, the gifts mentioned in verses 10–11 can only be exercised by those who have received them: by members of the fellowship gifted in those particular ways.

The charismatic/'renewal' movement has been largely responsible for reminding us of spiritual gifts and their importance. Today 'every-member ministry', where all play their part, is taught in many churches as a biblical ideal. Peter's teaching then is very relevant. What about these gifts?

Where are the gifts from? Their source is God himself, in his grace: any gift we have is 'received' (verse 10). Our gifts then don't come from us originally. Neither are they rewards for good behaviour – a Christian 'medal'. For our part, we are to be responsible stewards 'administering' our gifts properly. In practice this should remove pride in the use of our gifts: 'What do you have that you did not receive?' (1 Cor. 4:7). Also, for people to *use* their gifts there must presumably be some kind of 'recognition', the church and its leadership acknowledging people's God-given contributions. Space must be given for possible gifts to be tried out and eventually recognized or not. Finally, the use of gifts brings us back full-circle. God in his grace gives them, we use them (in his strength) and he receives the praise!

What kind of gifts are there? Peter answers this in two ways: firstly, God's grace is given in 'various forms' (verse 10): as a stained-glass window has but the one sun shining through it and yet gives a multitude of different effects, so is God's grace. Indeed, the list of twenty-six or so gifts mentioned in the New Testament (see *Spiritual Gifts*) is probably not complete. There are also various *kinds* of ministry, for example, those gifted as evangelists (Eph. 4:11): some are gifted with children, others with adults; one is able with large crowds and another with small groups. 'Various forms' of gifts (verse 10)!

Peter describes two kinds of gifts – speaking and doing (verse 11). Word and deed are both necessary and of equal importance for a fellowship to function properly.

Why are gifts given? Peter gives two reasons why God gives gifts: to 'serve others' (verse 10) and 'so that God may be praised' (verse 11). The use of our gifts may also bring a real sense of fulfilment to us although this is only a 'by-product'. Only one gift, tongues, is spoken of as ministering to *us* personally and directly (1 Cor. 14:4). So, by using our gifts to serve others the end-product is praise to God. Spiritual gifts then, are more like a 'towel' of service than a 'platform' of prominence!

How are our gifts to be used? They are to be used with a mixture of our responsibility and God's resources. We are the ones to 'use' our gifts – to 'do it' as Peter says twice (verse 11). His, however, are the resources: the words God provides in Scripture, and the strength God gives by his Spirit. Those with speaking gifts need to avoid being too casual or offhand in their preaching and teaching: they are handling what God says (verse 11)! People using gifts of service however, tend to be so practical that they run the risk of depending on their own energy. Organizing chairs for a service can be done without God – or can it? 'Servers' need to be wary of self-dependence! In both speaking and serving God is praised through Jesus Christ.

Praise results then from God's power (verse 11) working in the church – *graces* and *gifts* are included in the 'all things' (verse 11) for which he is praised. The whole section began in verse 7 with a triumphant statement about the 'end' being near, but there is *no* end to God's glory and power (verse 11)! Once again Peter lapses into worship.

Questions

1. *You ask someone in the church to give 'bed and breakfast' to a visiting speaker and their response is 'It's not my gift'! How would you correct their misunderstanding (using verses 7–11)?*

2. *What is your church's position on the use of spiritual gifts? (If in doubt, ask your minister or church leader.) Are you aware of where God has gifted you? How can you help others discover and develop their gifts?*

3. *What evidence is there of 'God at the centre' in these verses? Why do you think Peter sees praise as so important in the life of the church?*

Spiritual Gifts

The Greek term most commonly used in the New Testament for gifts is *charismata* (from which we get the term 'charismatic'). It literally means God's grace in action. In our own century, spiritual gifts have come more to the fore through the Pentecostal denominations, the charismatic/'renewal' movement, and the so-called 'new churches'.

Controversy has often surrounded the subject of gifts. Those following the teaching of a theologian called B.B. Warfield believe that most if not all the gifts mentioned in the New Testament are unavailable today. This is based on a misunderstanding of 1 Corinthians 13:10 that sees 'perfection' as the completion of the New Testament canon (collection of books) in the 4th century AD rather than the second coming of Christ. However, most Christians now accept that the twenty-six or so gifts are available for 'today'.

Gifts are outlined in three places outside our present passage. These 'lists' are found within the context of Paul's teaching on the church as the 'body'. They are: Romans 12:6–8; 1 Corinthians 12:8–10, 28; Ephesians 4:11. Clearly there is some overlap in these passages, with some gifts being mentioned more than once. The particular emphases of these three passages are: using our gifts because we have given our bodies to God (Romans); responding to God's grace in giving gifts by using them properly (Corinthians); equipping the whole church through gifts of 'people' (Ephesians).

32

1 Peter 4:12–13

Response to suffering – surprise or joy?

Suffering often catches us off guard. We don't always expect it. When it does come our reaction should not be one of surprise but one of joy.

Suffering for Christ is like a thread woven right throughout this letter. The suffering encountered was often verbal assault. A powerful form of insult is 'name calling' – poking fun at someone because of their name or that of someone they give allegiance to. Peter's readers were suffering for the second of these reasons: bearing the name of Christ (verses 14, 16).

Today, suffering for Christ often means receiving verbal abuse and it is as painful now as in Peter's day. In many countries the situation is worse, with Christians ostracized from their families, losing their jobs, and some forced to lay down their lives for Christ. How did Peter's readers respond in his day and what should have been their response?

First, it is good to realize exactly what we are going through and to face it squarely. Peter describes the experiences of his scattered Christian friends as 'the painful trial' (verse 12), or more literally in the Greek an experience of 'burning'.

This reminds us of his earlier teaching about trials that prove or test our faith like gold 'refined by fire' (1:7). Christian believers are not given automatic immunity from tough times, and the cost of discipleship is sometimes quite high. There is no exemption from the price of following Christ.

Second, these experiences have a way of confirming that our faith is real. In Jesus' parable of the soils the second type of soil, the shallow soil on rocky ground, is intriguing (Mk. 4:5–6, 16–17): people who seem to become Christians instantly and joyfully but who are only really 'a flash in the pan'. Trouble or persecution eventually shows them up for what they are: they are not the real thing! Conversely, Peter's encouragement is this: enduring through trials is one indication of the *genuineness* of our faith. Ultimately, there is no such thing as a 'fair weather Christian'.

How then should we react to painful trials such as constant verbal abuse, or indeed anything else we suffer for Christ's sake? Peter outlines two potential reactions: surprise or joy.

Surprise   For some reason, Peter's readers were 'caught off guard' by their trials. What was occurring to them seemed somehow out of the ordinary. Why? They were predominantly from Gentile backgrounds and whereas for Peter and his Jewish friends persecution was almost a way of life, Gentiles were not so familiar with this experience. For instance, in the case of the religions they had 'left behind', many of these were tolerated and often protected by Roman law. Now they were facing a definite *absence* of tolerance for Christ's sake. 'Live and let live' had become yesterday's slogan! Also, these believers were not used to suffering for doing the right thing: like many people in our society, they were well acquainted with punishment for wrong behaviour, but not for going God's way!

We too can sometimes view trials as 'surprise visitors', astonished to find them on our doorstep. This is especially true if we have not been warned of their arrival beforehand. However, Jesus clearly encountered painful trials, including verbal assault, and an integral part of our calling is to follow in his footsteps (2:21–23). We do not need to go looking for suffering, it will come to us provided we are not like salt that has lost its savour (Mt. 5:13). Jesus forewarned his disciples about suffering, indicating that they would have to follow him on that path (Mt. 5:11–12; Jn. 15:18–20) and, conversely, warned against people consistently heaping praise upon them (Lk. 6:26).

Joy   Peter's advice then is quite simple: 'Don't be surprised; do rejoice' (verse 12). Joy is to be one of the hallmarks of our salvation (1:8). Amazingly, our response to *suffering* is to be rejoicing. There are two reasons for this.

Firstly, in the here and now we 'participate in the sufferings of Christ' (verse 13). It is for *him* that we are suffering, and therefore we experience a real oneness with him in the process. What was designed to drive us away from him draws us closer to him. Our sense of solidarity with Jesus can actually be increased through these experiences. What grounds for joy (cf Acts 5:41)!

Secondly, we rejoice now because we look ahead to Christ's glory being 'revealed' at his second coming (verse 13). Then all our trials will be seen to have been worthwhile (1:7).

We are to leap for joy, then, not because we enjoy suffering for its own sake, but because of the closeness to Jesus that we experience in the process *and* because our joy will be multiplied when his glory is revealed.

Questions

1. *Why is it difficult to 'rejoice' in suffering? What does it mean? What doesn't it mean? How can you grow in this area?*

2. *Peter addresses his readers in the plural as 'friends' (verse 12). Within your church family how can Christians help each other to cope with, for example, the shock of suffering or suffering itself? What care do we need to take in encouraging others to 'rejoice' (verse 13) on these occasions?*

3. *What kinds of suffering do Christians experience in your culture and other parts of the world you have links with (for example, through friends, missionaries)? Why are there different forms of opposition in different places?*

Sharing Jesus' sufferings

Peter's readers 'participate in the sufferings of Christ' (verse 13). What does this mean? In one sense, Jesus' sufferings were unique: the death of a sinless person (1:19; 2:22) in a 'once for all' act (3:18) for our salvation. This is an impossible and unnecessary act to repeat!

Elsewhere though, Peter speaks of following the 'example' of Christ's sufferings (2:21) and arming ourselves with his 'attitude' (4:1).

Even this does not go deep enough though. Perhaps two examples will help us to understand what he is saying in verse 13.

Jesus was insulted during his lifetime (2:23). We are insulted because of him (4:14 etc.).

He was rejected by people at large (2:4). We are rejected and made to feel 'outsiders' because of him (4:4).

Suffering then is often a direct result of belonging to him and other people's response to that fact. The same theme comes out in Paul's teaching: for him and us 'the sufferings of Christ flow over into our lives' (2 Cor. 1:5) as well as our comfort now through Christ.

One question remains though: what about the suffering I experience that is *not* specifically for Christ's sake? For example, just because I'm human! Can I rejoice on these occasions too? Basically the answer is 'yes' because Jesus shared our humanity and can therefore help us in our suffering (Heb. 2:14, 18). He has already been through what we have, and can therefore be sympathetic (Heb. 4:15–16). So if, for example, we are deserted by close friends he understands and can help (NB: Mt. 26:31; 27:46). We can also rejoice because all such human suffering will end when 'his glory is revealed' (verse 13 cf Rev. 21:4).

33

1 Peter 4:14–16

Reason for suffering – Christ or evil?

Here Peter gives two reasons for our suffering. One is because we are Christians. The other is our own sin. Make sure it is the former and not the latter!

Having looked at two different responses to suffering, we now move on to tackle two different reasons for suffering in the first place. Peter is a wise, down to earth 'shepherd' (5:1–2) and realizes that some may misunderstand what he has been saying. They may think that any and every experience of suffering for the disciple is positive: that *all* suffering is to be rejoiced in regardless. One of the first questions we must ask though is: what are we or our fellow-Christians suffering for? For example, persecution at the factory may be because we are open about our faith when appropriate. Or it could be because we are constantly pushing our faith down other people's throats and misusing the firm's time in the process!

Suffering for Christ   What then, are the possible reasons behind our suffering? Legitimate suffering, says Peter, comes solely because we are linked to Christ and for no other reason. It is being 'insulted because of the name of Christ' (verse 14) and suffering 'as a Christian' (verse 16). The first expression does not mean being insulted because of a constant use of the name 'Jesus' in everyday speech. His name refers to all he is as a person, and so the insults come because of our *allegiance* to him. And the word 'Christian' in the first century had a different impact from our own day: it was a nickname for disciples of Jesus that was not always used positively (for example, Acts 26:28). From the world's perspective, being a 'Christian' is not an 'in' thing to be at all.

When we do experience suffering for the right reasons, there is great encouragement for us. First, there is the reality of the Holy Spirit's presence upon us (verse 14); second, unashamed witness goes out from us (3:15), and third, lively praise goes up from us to God (verse 16). Knowing that the third person of the Trinity is with us results in powerful worship and witness combined!

Suffering for evil

Some suffering, as we have hinted earlier, is *wrong* for the Christian believer and is not worthy to have the 'name of Christ' tagged on to it. Instead of saying something to the world around about Christ, everything it says is about us. If you suffer, then, says the apostle, make sure it is genuinely for Christ and not as a result of your own foolish behaviour (cf 2:20). For example, an employee can't claim to be suffering for Jesus when his wage packet is reduced because he arrives an hour late for work every day!

Two types of suffering, then, should be avoided by Christian disciples: things that are *legally* wrong and things that are *morally* wrong. Behaviour that could end us up behind bars and conduct that is plain anti-social.

If a Christian commits criminal acts such as murder or theft, he or she deserves to pay the price for such a lifestyle, in the same way that anyone would. A fine or a prison sentence is not 'persecution' in this context! Such misbehaviour as taking other people's money or property is forbidden for the Christian anyway (cf Eph. 4:28).

It is also possible to experience suffering because of anti-social conduct: for example, being a 'meddler' (verse 15) and interfering in other people's affairs. If we pry too much into the lives of others, and they respond negatively, we deserve what we get. The Bible's teaching on such occasions is blunt and uncompromising: 'mind your own business!' (1 Thess. 4:11; cf Jn. 21. 20–22).

Clearly, if we do engage in this kind of behaviour God can teach us something in the process: through lasting change, asking forgiveness and practising restitution where necessary (for example, giving back what we have wrongfully taken). However, we cannot label it 'suffering for Jesus'!

One of the first questions to ask of any experience of suffering is this: Why am I suffering? Is it because of faithfulness to Christ *or* as a result of my own sin? In helping fellow-Christians too, our counsel will be moulded by this truth: we must not indulge in a sense of 'Serves you right!' towards an erring brother or sister. However, we must be aware of the cause of their suffering, before advising them in how to handle it. If the initial diagnosis is wrong, incorrect medicine may be prescribed!

Questions

1. *If you suffer for the right reasons what will the eventual outcome be from God's angle and from your angle? How do you understand the phrase 'the Spirit ... rests on you' (verse 14)? What is the danger of being 'ashamed' (verse 16)?*

2. *Meddling (verse 15) is not a crime! Why is it wrong for the Christian? What effect could it have within a church fellowship (see for example, John 21:20–22)? Is 'live and let live' a good motto for a group of believers?*

3. *What does verse 15 imply about the legal system from God's perspective? How close, or otherwise, is yours to biblical principles (for example, the Ten Commandments)? In a democracy, how can Christians influence the law?*

The names 'Christ' and 'Christian'

Christians in Peter's day certainly faced 'name-calling'. They were branded because of their relationship with Christ. Both the names 'Christ' and 'Christian' were used in a negative way. Why are names important? Simply because in Scripture, and elsewhere sometimes, they sum up all that a person is (for example, Mt. 1:21).

From the early days the word 'Christian' was used by outsiders as a nickname for followers of Christ. King Agrippa certainly wasn't keen to become one (Acts 26:28)! Its use began in Antioch in present-day Syria (Acts 11:26). In Peter's day 'Christian' had an added impact: many religions, including Judaism, were permitted under Roman law, while Christianity was an 'illegal religion'. It was a crime to follow Jesus. Overall then, the apostle discourages his readers from being criminals ('murderer', thief' – verse 15) but realizes they are breaking the law by being Christians in the first place.

'Christ' literally means 'anointed one'. Here it is used of the person of Jesus, and it is the name we always carry or 'bear' (verse 16). His name is vital in conversion (Acts 2:21; Rom. 10:13), baptism (Mt. 28:19), prayer (Jn. 14:14; 16:24), service (Mk. 9:41) – in fact in *everything* (Col. 3:17).

One close parallel to this section in 1 Peter is Acts 5:41 which records the apostles rejoicing because of 'suffering disgrace for the Name' (cf further occurrences of 'name': Acts 5:28, 40).

34

1 Peter 4:17–19

Rightness of suffering – righteous or sinner?

God's judgment touches us all. It begins with existing family members. Outsiders experience it more forcefully later. Christian discipline should result in us committing ourselves to God and keeping on doing good.

Having highlighted the different responses to suffering and reasons for suffering, Peter turns our attention to the theme of judgment: for those within the family of God and non-Christians too. Both, in different ways, are subject to God's judgment, although they are clearly distinguished from each other too. So
why speak about judgment in the context of suffering (i.e. verses 12–19)? Probably because suffering is intended to have a purifying and disciplining effect on God's people (for example, 4:1).

To understand these somewhat difficult verses, it is important to realize that for the Christian 'judgment' is a present experience, whereas for the non-Christian it is primarily a future experience: 'What *will* the outcome be for those who do not obey the gospel of God?' (verse 17: author's italics). Probably, then, what Peter is referring to regarding Christians is 'discipline' as a form of judgment (cf Heb. 12:4 ff.). In a similar way Paul talks about the discipline of judgment now so that in future we will not be condemned along with the world (1 Cor. 11:32).

Judgment of Christians   For the Christian, then, judgment has been dealt with conclusively at the cross: 'He himself bore our sins in his body on the tree ... ' (2:24). However, that is not the whole story. Because our salvation has three tenses (see *Salvation – past, present and future* pp. 35–6) part of our 'being saved' involves God's discipline. Although we are firmly in the world, the world is not to be in us! Our privileges as members of the 'family of God' mean we are treated as legitimate children of God, on occasions experiencing the firmness of the Father's hand in our lives. This does not mean that he has ousted us from his family but rather that we are a genuine and much loved part of it (Heb. 12:6–7). Therefore, we need to recognize that God is *deeply* concerned about us being distinctive for him. If we refuse to share this passion he will use all manner of experiences to refine us.

Judgment for non-Christians   Judgment for non-Christians though, is going to be of a different order altogether, as shown by Peter's question in the second half of verse 18: 'what will become of the ungodly and the sinner?' Unlike Christians, who have 'obeyed the truth' (1:22), outsiders are guilty of disobeying God's gospel. The implication then, is that their future suffering will be of a far greater magnitude than the Christian's present discipline. They will have to give an account of their lives (4:5) without the 'defence counsel' of Jesus Christ to speak up for them! Peter underlines this by quoting from Proverbs 11:31: 'If the righteous receive their due on earth how much more the ungodly and the sinner!' The implication here is that the ungodly will receive a far greater return for their disobedience and sin at the *end* of their earthly lives.

In our daily lives, then, we as God's children should treat him with genuine reverence in the light of his role as the impartial judge of every human being (1:17), all the time realizing that we have been freed from his judgment through the death of Christ (1:18–19). We must also face with a sober attitude the awful destiny facing non-Christians, and be ready to give them a reason for the hope we have (3:15).

These verses, then, highlight the fact that God is Judge: both of Christian (1:17) and non-Christian (4:5). For us as believers this means 'discipline' in this life to aid us in sharing his character (1:15–16). Part of this process is experiencing tough times for doing the right thing, and sometimes even the wrong thing!

To recap briefly, there are two questions we must ask of any experience of suffering:

What is our response to it?
Do we greet it with shock or with joy (verses 12–13)?

What is the reason for it?
Are we suffering for Christ or for our own evil (verses 14–16)?

If we have answered these questions properly, how can we find that measure of joy described in verse 13? What do we actually *do* when suffering 'according to God's will' (verse 19)? Peter gives the answer in the same verse.

Like Jesus himself (2:23), we should commit ourselves to our 'faithful Creator'. God will consistently take care of our lives. Peter also realizes that we may be tempted to give up the distinctive lifestyle of the Christian because of the cost entailed and take the way of least resistance. 'No', says Peter: 'Keep up the good work'.

Questions

1. *What are the alternatives to following Peter's advice in verse 19? How else could you be tempted to respond? Have you ever felt like 'throwing in the towel' when suffering? Why? What did you do?*

2. *Why does Peter describe the church as 'the family of God' in verse 17? How does this help us in understanding God's discipline? What is the difference between judgment for Christians and non-Christians?*

3. *What is the destiny of those who do not obey the gospel (see, for example, 2 Pet. 2:4–9; 3:7 cf 2 Thess. 1:5–10)? How does the average non-Christian respond to this? What would you say in answer to the accusation: 'It's not fair!'?*

Discipline of Christians

Two Old Testament passages in particular lie behind
verse 17. First, in Ezekiel 9, where judgment starts at
the Temple sanctuary (verse 6), and proceeds outwards. In fact, the prophecy of Ezekiel as a whole
involves the judgment of God's people (chapters 4 – 24)

before the other nations (chapters 25 – 32). Second, in Malachi 3, where
the Lord comes near his people for judgment (verse 5): this involves
refining his people so that they can offer him acceptable sacrifices
(verses 3–4).

In the New Testament there are two other passages warranting further study.

1. In Paul's teaching on 'communion' in 1 Corinthians 11:17–34, he
   speaks of examining ourselves before taking the Lord's Supper in
   order to avoid God having to discipline us (verse 31) and to avoid
   being condemned along with the world (verse 32).
2. In Hebrews 12:4–13 the writer outlines the value of God's 'discipline' stressing that discipline shows we really are God's children
   (verses 5–8), and that his long-term goal for us through discipline is
   holiness (verses 10–11).

In 1 Peter the aim of 'discipline' is clear – that we might share God's
holy character (1:15–16). God's discipline for believers results in
growth and blessing but his discipline for unbelievers results in judgment and hell. As an impartial judge (1:17) God begins with believers –
those who 'know' (1:18), not the ignorant (1:14). Knowledge brings
responsibility. Then his judgment continues with unbelievers (4:5: see
Second chance after death?).

GRACE FOR CHRISTIANS AT DIFFERENT STAGES
1 Peter 5:1–7

35

1 Peter 5:1–4

Leadership in the church

Good leaders are essential in the church. They will care for people and co-ordinate the ministry, all from the right motives. For such leaders there is an amazing incentive for serving.

Vital to the health of any church is the quality of its leadership, especially when its members are experiencing difficulties! Peter introduces this new theme sandwiched between two sections that focus largely on suffering. There are two possible reasons for this.

First, pressure on any group can eventually make it come apart at the seams. Leaders are often the first to be attacked! Peter may, then, be encouraging solidarity in the church while it is experiencing pressure.

Second (and more likely) the apostle has just spoken about 'discipline' beginning with God's family (4:17–19). It will probably start initially with the *leaders* of that family (cf Ezk. 9:6). Discipline calls for real purity of heart in the church and leaders are to set the pace in this as good 'examples' (verse 3).

In this discussion of leadership should those who are *not* leaders switch off at this point, as single people could in the discussion on marriage (3:1–7) or husbands in the discussion on the role of wives (3:1–6)? No! The whole church should be concerned about leadership because of the impact of leaders on the church 'for better or for worse'. Guidelines about the choice of leaders and how to pray for them should be matters of concern for us all.

'Elders' (verse 1) are called to serve not just because of age and experience, but because of spiritual maturity. Sometimes these go together, but not always. They are to be a real *part* of the family, being 'among you' (verse 1), not just guiding and leading God's people from a safe distance! After all, how can they be 'examples' if their lifestyle is never observed?

Peter counts himself a 'fellow-elder' with them (verse 1), yet he introduces himself at the start of his letter as the authoritative 'apostle' (1:1). Why the change here? Simply because as 'a pastor to the pastors' he genuinely wants to get *alongside* them. Dictatorial orders from on high would not help and genuine fellowship would be lost. Also, with his high standards for elders (verses 2–4), Peter may want them to know that he realizes personally what it is to fail and be restored (Jn. 21:15 ff).

Unlike the other 'elders', Peter was a firsthand witness of Jesus' sufferings. Nevertheless, his fellow elders knew something of sharing in Christ's sufferings now (4:13) as did the whole congregation. But when Jesus returns triumphant they will all share together in his glory. Faithful elders will even receive 'a crown of glory', some kind of special reward in heaven for their service (verse 4).

The job description of church leaders is twofold: to be shepherds and overseers (verse 2), following in the footsteps of Jesus 'the Shepherd and Overseer of your souls' (2:25).

Shepherds   The appointment of 'Shepherds' in the church is a fulfilment of God's promises concerning leadership in the Old Testament (Je. 3:15; 23:4, etc.). Peter himself was called to a shepherding role following his restoration (Jn. 21:16). There are two particular characteristics of shepherds. First, the personal care of the shepherd for the sheep: for example, he knows them individually by name (Jn. 10:3). Spiritual shepherds do not treat their flock as an impersonal 'list', but are aware of the details of their lives (job, family, spiritual history, etc.). Second, it is not the shepherd's flock but *God's*! Jesus is the 'Chief Shepherd' (verse 4). Therefore, the care of God's people is given to elders on trust. Believers don't belong to their leaders, but to God and so elders cannot ultimately call them 'my people'.

Overseers   The title of 'overseers' is perhaps less familiar. The idea is one of a superintendent at work, whose task is one of co-ordination, making sure jobs are done, etc. It is someone who can see the whole picture, and how the parts fit together too: rather like a site manager on a building site, perched high above the actual construction level and, therefore, having an overall perspective. Church 'overseers' see clearly from *above* to serve humbly *below*.

'Elders' then are to be characterized by personal care and overall co-ordination. They should be intimately involved in people's lives without losing sight of the whole picture. But what fuel of motivation are they running on? Peter answers this by looking at three kinds of attitude all introduced with the formula 'not ... but' (verses 2b–3).

'not because you must, but because you are willing' (verse 2)

The first motivation is that of a wrong kind of obligation: 'I'm doing it because I have to'. God's people must be wary of press-ganging people into positions of leadership. Volunteers should not emerge solely because 'Someone has to do the job!' Healthy motivation is a key sign of an elder's calling for Paul too (1 Tim. 3:1). The Chief Shepherd is not looking for grudging conscripts, but for willing volunteers!

'not greedy for money, but eager to serve' (verse 2)

A second attitude concerns money. Some elders in New Testament times were released from their jobs to serve the church full-time and were rightly paid for it (1 Tim. 5:17–18; cf Lk. 10:7). However, a salary cheque at the end of the month is not the *reason* for serving! A leader's motivation should be quite different from the false teachers, who made up 'fairy tales' for material gain (2 Pet. 2:3). Leaders then must be wary of 'milking' their congregations.

'not lording it over those entrusted to you, but being examples' (verse 3)

Hankering after power is the third attitude to avoid. In the everyday world people often get to the top by being domineering and pushy. This 'lording it over' people though, is not to be found in the church where there is but *one* Lord (1:3; 3:15). There should be no force or manipulation on the part of Christian leaders. Christians, of course, will more gladly follow someone whose lifestyle is an attractive example – who doesn't 'shove it down their throats'!

If leaders are not to serve unwillingly or for money or power, what are the incentives that will spur them on to lead the flock gladly and well? Peter uses the example of the award given to athletes in Greek and Roman times: the winner was crowned with a wreath of laurel leaves. In like manner, elders will 'receive the crown of glory' from the Chief

Shepherd (verse 4). The leader's reward is primarily spiritual, a 'crown of glory', and is permanent: 'will never fade away'. Perhaps surprisingly then, there is an incentive for serving well in the church although a reward that has to be waited for. It will be given when 'the Chief Shepherd appears' (verse 4).

Questions

1. *As someone involved in a local church, how can you play your part in helping your leaders be all that God intended? Are there any hints here about how to support/pray for them and their families (where appropriate)?*

2. *Twice Peter mentions future 'glory' when speaking about church leadership (verses 1 and 4). Why was this important then? Why is it vital for leaders now? What difference should a long-term perspective make?*

3. *How does the Christian 'leadership style' differ from leadership in the world at large (for example, business management, political leadership, etc)? Are there any similarities? What insights can we learn about Christian leadership from the shepherd-flock picture?*

36

1 Peter 5:5-7

Humility in the church

Unchecked pride ruins a fellowship. God's desire is humility for *every* Christian, but particularly the younger generation. His grace and care are experienced by anyone willing to learn this lesson.

The leaders have just been addressed by Peter as fellow leaders. He now returns to the whole church family and to the familiar theme of submission: towards our fellow-Christians and to God himself.

Submission – younger to older The apostle first calls the 'young men' (or possibly 'young people') to attention! They are to be submissive probably to the 'elders' rather than 'those who are older' (as NIV). The dividing line between 'young men' and 'those who are older' is not completely clear: for example Timothy was described as 'young' (1 Tim. 4:12) when in his early to mid thirties. Whatever the case most church leaders were probably in the upper-age bracket. So why this instruction? Perhaps there was a situation where the 'generation gap' was widening with younger people thinking they knew better and should have a greater say in the running of the church, and older people feeling threatened! Young people can often be independent-minded and sometimes rebellious. Therefore, they may need a special reminder. This is especially relevant in Western culture today, where there is a tendency to idolize youth and downplay older people. However, in defence of younger Christians, a wise group of elders will ensure that their views are taken into account and that their leadership capabilities are increasingly fostered and developed.

Submission – everyone to everyone

Next, the whole church (scattered though it was!) is issued with a charge to humility. *All* age groups need to learn this lesson. It should characterize our relationships with every member of God's family.

Firstly then, we are responsible for humbling ourselves (verses 5 and 6): no other human being can do it for us.

Secondly, the ultimate reason for humility is not found in our relationships with each other, but in God's response to the humble. Those who consider themselves 'the great I am' he tends to pull down. Others, who are willing to recognize their genuine need of God, are provided with grace (Pr. 3:34). This is completely at odds with the popular way of 'getting on': the proud going further up the ladder, and the humble increasingly downtrodden. God's kingdom is an 'upside-down kingdom'!

People's clothing says a lot about them: 'clothe yourselves' (verse 5). Their dress reveals a great deal about their personalities. In our personalities and characters how are we clothed in relation to our brothers and sisters: with humility or pride?

From these two instructions to 'younger men' and to 'all of you' we can learn a great deal. Harmony within any church fellowship is dependent on the way people treat one another and the starting point is our attitudes; in fact *my* attitude. A church under pressure then, will be held together by caring, co-ordinating leaders (verses 1–4) and by the humble attitudes of all God's people (verses 5–6).

Submission – Christians to God

Being only human, some Christians find it difficult to submit to others in the family – whether as led to leaders or as Christian to fellow-Christian. This may indicate a deeper problem, for example, doubting the loving character of God and therefore finding it difficult to humble themselves before him. Looked at from the opposite angle: those who *have* learnt to submit to him will not find it such a problem to be humble towards other Christians. Peter emphasizes the importance of humility in verse 5 by quoting Proverbs 3:34: God 'gives grace to the humble'. We need therefore, to submit ourselves to God in everyday experience. Scripture must be 'earthed' in practice. If not, we may find God humbling us from the 'opposition benches'! We are also to humble ourselves 'under God's mighty hand' (verse 6) which probably refers to the way God exercises discipline in the lives of his people (for example, see Job 30:21). If this is correct, the implication is that Peter's readers should 'bear up' under persecution. Rather than fighting back against their enemies or blaming God, they should see the hand of God in it all.

Being humble, though, is not the same as being humiliated! This is not God's way for the submissive. Those learning to yield to him know that 'promotion' is on its way. Jesus' death (3:18) was followed by his resurrection/ascension (3:21–22). Our steps 'down' will be followed by a God-given lift 'up'.

Coping with anxiety is somehow linked to being humble for Peter as verses 6 and 7 form *one* sentence in the original Greek. Dealing with worry then, is a practical outworking of the command to be humble. What is the connection? People learning to practise humility toward others may wonder: 'But who will look after *me*?'. The answer is God himself: he is both able ('mighty hand': verse 6) and willing ('he cares': verse 7) to make our concerns his! And his care is ongoing, not every now and then. Giving our worries back to him frees us from thinking too much about ourselves, and helps us to consider others more.

So 'cast all your anxiety on him' (verse 7). What are we leaving with him? We should give him any worries or concerns that weigh us down heavily (cf Ps. 55:22). The devil delights to play on our anxieties (verse 8), but our God is well able to carry them (verse 7). What are you waiting for?

Questions

1. Describe 'humility' in your own words. How would you recognize it? What signs would you look for in assessing growth in humility in yourself and others?

2. What are relationships across the 'age-divide' like in your church? How could fellowship between younger and older be improved? Why will humility be needed? Is Peter unfair on younger people?

3. What are the main causes of anxiety in today's world? In what different ways do people try to alleviate their worries? Does Peter's advice to Christians (verse 7) relate to personal issues only or to global issues too?

The 'generation gap'

In verse 5 Peter highlights the difference between 'young men' and 'those who are older' (or 'elders' as in verses 1–4). Some believe that 'young men' refers to a specific ministry in the early church (as for example, in Acts 5:6, 10): almost a 'trainee' status. This is not certain however, but what *is* fascinating is the way the apostles face the reality of 'age differentials'.

Peter openly acknowledges differences of age in his 'Pentecost' sermon (Acts 2:17): young men and old men experience slightly different gifts from the Holy Spirit.

Paul speaking to the young man Timothy gives specific instructions regarding relationships with younger and older people of both sexes (1 Tim. 4:12; 5:1–2). Roles and ministries too are influenced by age considerations, the older Christians 'discipling' the younger ones (Tit. 2:1–8).

John outlines different 'stages' of spirituality for children, young men, and fathers (1 Jn. 2:12–14).

For Peter in this letter, unity is paramount regardless of age. Love spans the whole family. Only humble attitudes though, can prevent the generation gap from widening. These issues need careful thought at a time where 'youth services' and complete 'youth churches' are being experimented with and where integration of different age-groups is sometimes difficult to achieve within the local church.

GRACE FOR CHRISTIANS IN DIFFERENT SITUATIONS
1 Peter 5:8–14

37

1 Peter 5:8–9

Warfare in the church

Christians are on active service. Their opponent is the devil himself. He can be defeated by our steady faith and by realizing that we are not on our own.

'Lion at liberty' ran the headline of a newspaper near an English zoo recently! As a result, many people in the surrounding towns and villages were very much on their guard.

Here Peter openly introduces the devil for the first time, picturing him as 'a roaring Lion' (verse 8). He is at war with Christians, but their God is 'the God of all grace' (verse 12). *He* will be on their side in the battle! Although the devil is only mentioned by name at this stage of the letter his presence has been implicit throughout, for example, when Peter lists evil desires (4:2–4) and discusses suffering (3:8–12). Behind persecution from 'flesh and blood' people is an unseen 'commander-in-chief', the devil. The instigator of verbal flak from non-Christians is the 'accuser of our brothers' (Rev. 12:10).

Who is the devil? Firstly, he is our 'enemy' (cf Satan: a Hebrew word meaning 'enemy') who prowls around like a hungry lion seeking to catch and eat whatever comes across his path (verse 8: cf Ps. 22:13). He can either confront us in the open with a fierce, intimidating roar (verse 8) or can hide in the long grass, concealed and ready to pounce (cf Ps. 10:9).

Secondly, he is the 'devil' (from the Greek word *diabolos* meaning to slander). The term is used of an opponent or adversary in the law courts, arguing the case against the prisoner in the dock. The devil's strategy is to blacken our name before God through the use of slander and then to tempt us to doubt that God proclaims we are holy in his sight through the cleansing blood of Jesus. This truth is strongly affirmed by, for example, Paul in Romans 5:9a .

What are the devil's aims? He is 'looking for someone to devour' (verse 8). Devouring conjures up the picture of a bird of prey drinking its victim down whole! His desire is nothing less than to 'do away with us' and he is prepared to use any methods. For Peter's readers, this probably meant being tempted to deny their faith altogether. For the elders (verses 1–4) it may have meant being 'put out of action', for example, because of sexual sin or financial misconduct. Christians nowadays are not immune either: an attacked faith can easily become a wobbly faith, and a fall could be just round the corner. The devil's aim is to inflict as many casualties as he can, despite the fact that the final outcome of the war is never in doubt. He *will* be beaten (Rev. 20:10).

The surest way of winning any battle is to catch the enemy off guard either when he is least expecting it or when he is battle-weary and tired. Because of this, we are to be 'self-controlled and alert' (verse 8) at all times. We need to be like soldiers on a battlefield always ready for duty (cf Eph. 6:10–18). Jesus himself emphasized these qualities in relation to the difficulties facing Christians before his return (Mk. 13:32–37). Don't be caught 'napping'!

How should we respond to the devil? We should respond to the devil by resisting him! For Christians the devil *is* resistible! As we say a firm 'No' he takes to his heels (Jas. 4:7). Interestingly, there are no 'techniques' of spiritual warfare mentioned here (for example, prayer-walking and 'binding' spirits), just the encouragement that we can triumph!

Peter also suggests that we can win the battle against the devil without even moving but by 'standing firm in the faith' spiritually (cf Eph. 6:13–14). The devil's aim is to shift us from the terrain of trusting God. In the heat of the battle then, we are to dig our heels in, not yielding ground taken so far.

Encouragement in battle Why should we be encouraged in the battle? In any war there is strength in numbers! An isolated soldier faces more temptation to wave the white flag of surrender than a battalion does. We can cope better with the scars of battle if we know we are not the only ones taking part. Peter's encouragement then is that 'your brothers throughout the world are undergoing the same kind of sufferings' (verse 9). In other words 'Other Christians are going through what you are'. In today's world suffering for believers in one country may be quite different from that in another. However, there is a price to pay for our faith whatever part of the globe we live in.

Warfare of course involves plenty of grazes on the way. Some Christians are like the 'walking wounded' – physically fit perhaps, but spiritually maimed. The good news, though, is this: while the devil's aim is to 'take us apart', God's aim is to 'restore' us (verse 10) and put us together again. Casualties are not discarded in this war! So, Peter encourages Christians under siege in three ways:

- the devil is resistible (verse 9a)
- you are not on your own (verse 9b)
- the end is in sight (verse 10).

Questions

1. *What is the devil trying to do with Christians? How do you think he has been attacking you or your church recently? Give practical examples of what it means to 'resist' him.*

2. *Why is fellowship so important in the spiritual battle? How can it help us 'fight on' when the going gets tough? Are there any isolated Christians locally you could encourage?*

3. *How aware are you of suffering Christians 'throughout the world'? Are there organisations through whom you could learn more? Could you/your church help in any particular situations? How?*

Spiritual Warfare

Peter says little else in his letter about 'spiritual war-fare': that is our battle against the devil and his demons that can affect every aspect of our lives, spiritually, mentally, physically and so on. The only exceptions are the reference to 'angels, authorities and powers' being in submission to the ascended Jesus (3:22) and the devil as 'slanderer' revealing his true colours through the verbal abuse of non-Christians (cf 5:8 and 3:16).

There are two parallel passages to 5:8–9 in the New Testament:

James 4:7 Like Peter, James locates his teaching on the devil right after emphasizing submission to God and also quotes Proverbs 3:34. A vital addition is the idea of the devil fleeing if we resist him: 'Resist the devil and he will flee from you' (Jas. 4:7)! Significantly, James'passage is very *God-centred* in emphasis, avoiding the danger of giving too much attention to the opposition! Jesus, of course, gave us a good 'model' for resisting Satan when he was tempted in the wilderness (Lk. 4:1–13).

Ephesians 6:10–20 Here Paul likens our resistance to the devil in terms of warfare, the soldier being kitted out in spiritual armour in order to be protected from and resist being overcome by the devil. An important link here is the emphasis of both Peter and Paul on 'stand-ing' firm against the enemy (5:9 cf Eph. 6:11, 13, 14). Obviously one of Satan's aims is to get us to yield ground spiritually by attempted intim-idation (cf 1 Pet. 3:14b).

Essential to our warfare is a clear understanding of the devil's defeat which was accomplished through Jesus' death (Col. 2:15; Heb. 2:14) and his resurrection/ascension (Eph. 4:8, cf 3:21–22). Because of Jesus' conquest any battle we engage in is 'out *from* victory' rather than 'for-ward *to* victory'!

38

1 Peter 5:10–14

God of all grace

Suffering Christians need to be sure of God's grace and power. He will soon heal all their battle wounds. Meanwhile, they are to express God's grace to each other and know his peace.

The smell of battle is still in the air as Peter finishes off his letter. Spiritual warfare is fierce but it is possible to win through by faith (verses 8–9). Three particular dangers face anyone in a war situation: losing sight of the Commanding Officer; struggling along when 'war-wounded'; and wondering if the battle will ever end.

Peter knew each of these dangers first-hand. He had taken his eyes off the Commanding Officer once when he was walking on the lake towards Jesus (Mt. 14:28–31). As a result he began to sink and was saved only through turning his attention back to Jesus and holding onto his hand.

Later on the battle-weary Peter denied Jesus three times and became a broken man spiritually (Lk. 22:54–62). However, after Jesus was resurrected he restored his wounded soldier, Peter, and returned him to the 'front line' (Jn. 21:15–17). From his own personal experience then Peter can write assuring his friends that the battle will end soon and final victory is in sight (verse 10).

Peter addresses three questions about our God which are relevant to this war situation.

Who is he?   He is 'the God of all grace' (verse 10). He is not like the devouring lion whose aim is to inflict maximum damage on us (verse 8) but is more akin to the art-restorer who lovingly brings a damaged painting back to its real 'glory' (verse 10). Peter describes God as 'the God of all grace' to remind us that all his generous gifts, in particular our salvation, are given without any reference to how we have treated him. All grace is from God and he is able to meet us with grace precisely at *our* point of need, whatever the situation! He also takes direct personal responsibility for his children's welfare: he 'will himself restore you' (verse 10). Why is this truth so vital? Because Christians facing suffering can sometimes view God in a distorted way, for example, as someone who 'enjoys' seeing them suffer. As the God of all grace he *doesn't*! So, keep your eyes on his gracious character, especially in the heat of battle.

What has he called us to?   He has called us to 'eternal glory in Christ': this is the realm in which we shall see God's character shining out completely and perfectly. Naturally we may shrink back in awe from entering such territory, but we are welcomed as those 'in Christ', believers united with him. It is primarily *his* glory that will be revealed (4:13). However, faithful leaders will share in it (5:1, 4) and every Christian is called to experience it (verse 10).

Believers then and now experience real 'knocks' in this life. How are we to be prepared for this 'eternal glory'? God himself will make us ready in four related ways: He will

- 'restore you': any damage done to us will be fully repaired
- 'make you strong': our weaknesses will be replaced by strength
- 'make you ... firm': wobbly Christians will be able to stand secure
- 'make you ... steadfast': we will all be placed on a sure foundation.

In summary, every single battle scar will be healed for all eternity (verse 10).

When will this happen?   Peter says that we will be restored 'after ... a little while' (verse 10). Suffering produces character in this life (Rom. 5:3–5) if we respond to it correctly. The main emphasis *here*, though, is on our final restoration after short-term suffering: pain for 'a little while' contrasted with 'eternal glory' to come (verse 10). The knocks of life will always leave us with a partial 'limp', but complete wholeness, through Christ, is on its way!

We can be sure of this because God has endless resources: 'power for ever and ever' (verse 11) to produce Christlikeness in us 'now' and to save us completely 'then'. Our response should be a heartfelt 'Yes Lord! Amen'.

So, because of his character, all God's intentions for us are gracious ones (verse 10). More than that, he gives us 'the true grace of God' (verse 12). This is the theme of Peter's entire letter: *grace*! Grace is God showing us his favour when we clearly do not deserve it. It is demonstrated most profoundly in Jesus dying for us 'the righteous for the unrighteous' (3:18). From our angle we experience God's grace when we first become Christians. However, even in the here and now we need to 'stand in it' before God and 'live in it' with others (verses 12–14).

Standing in grace   The 'true grace of God' rests on what he has done for us in Christ, not what we have done for him. It is *safe* ground because of that! However, Peter is aware that we can move from our position in grace. Tough times may cause us to shift from 'grace' because we begin to doubt his love and care. Or our hope of receiving 'grace' at Jesus' return (1:13) begins to 'flag'. Non-Christians too may attempt to move us from 'grace', pushing us to return to our previous lifestyle (4:1–4). Grace, then, is to 'stand fast in' (cf Rom. 5:2).

The Galatian Christians were being shifted from grace by 'legalists' who were trying to make them live by the Jewish laws instead of living by God's grace. Peter's readers however, were tempted to move from grace through being 'under fire' from the *outside* world. The apostle's advice was to avoid being dislodged from gospel-ground!

Living in grace   Grace is not only to stand in. It is to be lived in too: in relation to our fellow-Christians *and* in a practical way. This grace is worked out in our relationships with other believers. God's grace had united Peter's readers with the church in Rome, described here as 'she who is in Babylon' (verse 13). It had also linked them to individuals such as Silas (verse 12) and Mark (verse 13). Grace can be seen here in four ways:

1. Helping one another. Silas assisted Peter in his correspondence (verse 12: cf 1 Thess. 1:1; 2 Thess. 1:1) probably helping with 'secretarial skills'. In Peter's day many people could neither read nor write, so a scribe would write and read letters for those who could not do so. Alternatively Silas may have carried the letter to its destination.

2. Encouraging one another. Peter's main purpose in writing was to encourage his readers in their tough, lonely situation, by reminding them of God's grace (verse 12).
3. Greeting one another. Both the Roman Christians and Mark sent greetings in this letter to Peter's friends. Believers in Asia Minor were to greet one another physically with a 'kiss of love' (verse 14; cf 1 Thess. 5:26), an affectionate Christian hug to make God's grace *felt* among them.
4. Blessing one another. Peter finishes as he began by blessing his readers with God's 'peace' (verse 14; cf 1:2), not just as a formality but rather praying it for them once again!

So grace is to be expressed from Christian to Christian and from church to church: showing God's generous heart to one another in tangible and 'down to earth' ways.

Peter's letter reaches its finale with some beautiful descriptions of God in relation to ourselves: 'the God of all grace' (verse 10) to restore us and the 'true grace of God' (verse 12) to stand in and live in. He ends with a blessing for all Christians then and now: 'Peace to all of you ...' (verse 14).

As those 'in Christ' we can know a real measure of tranquillity, even when we are going through tough times. Praise God!

Questions

1. *How aware are you of being part of a world-wide church (see verse 13)? What can we do to 'build bridges' with fellowships in other countries? Why is this important for churches whose suffering is especially great right now?*

2. *What can we learn here about real fellowship? How is it to be experienced? Do we need safeguards in showing love physically (verse 14)? If so, what? How could fellowship in your church be improved?*

3. *Are you standing in God's grace now? How do you know whether you are or not? What tempts you to move from it?*

Babylon

Whatever the location of 'Babylon' it is clear that Peter brings greetings from a church there. The clues are the use of the feminine 'she', hinting at the church as Christ's bride (cf Eph. 5:25–27); and the remark 'chosen together with you' which seems to refer to all Christians (cf 1:2) rather than just an individual.

There are three possibilities as to the location of 'Babylon':

Babylon in Mesopotamia   This is unlikely because we have no evidence of a church there or of Peter visiting the region. Although Babylon played a major role in the Old Testament as an invading nation, by the first century AD the city of Babylon was a small, obscure place, fast becoming a ghost-town.

Babylon in Egypt   This was the site of a Roman garrison near Old Cairo. The Christian writer Eusebius indicates that Mark (cf verse 13) had a hand in founding the church in Egypt.

Against this view, though, there is no evidence to link Peter with Egypt. Also Mark apparently ventured only as far south as Alexandria and no further.

Rome in Italy   Babylon as a metaphor for Rome makes most sense for three reasons:

First, we know from the writings of the Christian authors Tertullian (AD 203) and Eusebius (AD 325) that the apostle Peter was based in Rome at the time this letter was written (AD 62–64). It is quite likely then that in verse 13 Peter is sending greetings from his home church at the heart of the empire.

Second, Babylon was already used as a metaphor for Rome by three sets of writers: the Jews (for example in the *Sybilline Oracles* and 2 *Baruch*); the Christians (for instance in Revelation 14:8; 17:5; 18:2), and the Romans (some of whom apparently referred to Rome as 'another Babylon' because of its decadence).

Third, this explanation fits in well with Peter's use of Old Testament images in his letter (for example describing the church in terms reminiscent of God's people Israel). Babylon in the Old Testament was the centre of the then-known world, a place of luxury and sin, and a focus of opposition to God's people. Its natural equivalent in the first century AD would have been Rome.

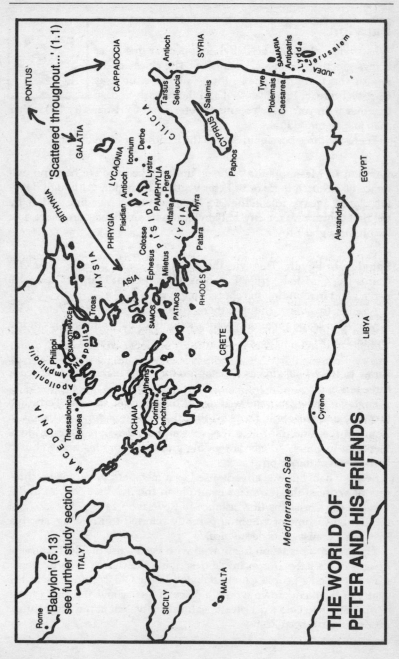

THE WORLD OF
PETER AND HIS FRIENDS

'Scattered throughout...' (1.1)

'Babylon' (5.13)
see further study section

For further reading

1 Peter is well served by good commentaries. For those who want to study the letter in greater depth the following are recommended:

A 'heavyweight' commentary that includes the original Greek but is also readable is the recent one by P.H. Davids (*New International Commentary on the New Testament*, Eerdman's 1990).

At a middle level the work by W. Grudem (*Tyndale New Testament Commentary*, Inter-Varsity Press 1988) is exceptionally helpful. A popular level commentary that is written in conversational style is *Be Hopeful* by W.W. Wiersbe (Scripture Press 1988).

Probably the most helpful all-round commentary though is that written by I.H. Marshall (*IVP New Testament Commentary Series*, Inter-Varsity Press 1991). This combines good exegesis (understanding the meaning of the text) with down-to-earth application of 1 Peter to today's world.